Joy NOTES

*Balancing
the Trauma
with Triumph*

NIOBIS QUEIRO

JOY NOTES: Balancing the Trauma with Triumph
Copyright ©2024 Niobis Queiro

All Rights Reserved.

No part of this publication may be reproduced, stored in a retrieval system or transmitted, in any form or by any means—electronic, mechanical, photocopying, recording, or otherwise—without prior written permission from the publisher, except for the inclusion of brief quotations in a review.
For information about this title or to order other books and/or electronic media, contact the publisher:

Two Sisters Writing & Publishing®
TwoSistersWriting.com
18530 Mack Avenue, Suite 166
Grosse Pointe Farms, MI 48236

Hardcover ISBN 978-1-956879-51-3
Paperback ISBN 978-1-956879-52-0
EBook ISBN 978-1-956879-53-7

Printed in the United States of America
All the stories in this work are true.
Cover and Graphic Design: Illumination Graphics.
Author photos: The Queiro Collection.

WHAT PEOPLE ARE SAYING ABOUT NIOBIS QUEIRO

"In *Joy Notes*, Nio Quiero composes an anthem to life, written in the keys of resilience and grace. Her most remarkable book, which begins in Cuba and spans 50-plus years as she rises through losses and even death itself, to become a mother, wife, and executive—as a woman on a path with purpose and heart. Her stories are testaments to the enduring power of music and the human spirit to overcome and uplift, to find joy and call others to the dance. If you need to be reminded of the courage and joy that lies within you, pick up this book and let its melodies work on your heart."

—**Malynn Utzinger**
Director of Integrative Practices at Promega

"Nio, you truly are an incredible person! I am absolutely amazed to learn that you have not only encountered the Matrix, but have emerged victorious from its depths. I am grateful for your generosity in sharing an excerpt from your book, which serves as a powerful testament to your unwavering resilience. Your ability to confront obstacles head-on and bounce back stronger than ever is truly remarkable. The memories of our time together at GNYHA remain vivid, and I feel incredibly fortunate to have crossed paths with someone as extraordinary as you, even if our time together was fleeting.

Each of us embarks on a unique life journey, and it is during the pivotal moments that we can either succumb to the challenges or, like you, rise above them, dust ourselves off, and embrace the potential opportunities that lie ahead. Let us raise a toast to the better days that await us all. Remember, it's not over until the fat lady sings . . ."

— **Cesar Limjoco, M.D.**
Chief Medical Officer, Board Advisor, Keynote Speaker
T-Medicus LLC

JOY NOTES

"Work-life balance is so vitally important for us to have true happiness and joy. Still, realistically, it is hard to achieve, especially when you have social and economic obstacles of being an immigrant and a person of color, while your family is having difficult medical conditions in tandem with your health issues.
In Nio's book, *Joy Notes: Balancing the Trauma with Triumph*, we get a close, intimate view of how she navigates the complexities of life using her resilient spirit, humor, tenacity, and MUSIC.

Her multifaceted story touches on various topics, such as health equity, professionalism within the corporate world, the family dynamic, and learning how to reach out to friends for help. The book is a guide to help those in professional spaces, but it is more than that. It is a victorious story of someone who would not let anything stop her from living her best life. There is so much inspiration packed in the pages, you will not be disappointed.

I highly recommend this book to everyone, and I say buy one for a friend. They will thank you for it, because we all need a friend like Nio who will cheer you on, no matter what.
Her essence is just that powerful and transcends the pages of the book and jumps into your heart like the *Joy Notes* of your favorite tune."

—**Vicquita Renee**
Health Equity Program Coordinator
Healthcare Management Consultant
Government Program Analyst
Grievance & Appeals Coordinator
Partnership HealthPlan of California

"Nio is such a gifted storyteller and is able to seamlessly weave the experiences from her life together to provide incredible wisdom! Even though much of the book is focused on women, I found myself often relating to her stories and took away so much guidance for myself that I can apply to my life. Women AND men will enjoy this book and certainly benefit from the many *Joy Notes!*"

—**Ryan Gibson**
Managing Director
Huron Consulting Group

WHAT PEOPLE ARE SAYING

"Notes can be lonely until an artist crafts them into a song. Words have no context until an author organizes them into a story. Niobis Queiro is both an artist and an author who has the incredible ability to conjure music and words into the spellbinding narrative of her life. I have had the privilege of being a friend and colleague of Nio's for nearly two decades. In that time, I have had the honor of witnessing her achieve incredible professional successes and overcome life-threatening tragedies while inspiring countless women, healthcare professionals, and audiences across the country.

JOY NOTES: Balancing the Trauma with Triumph is the remarkable ballad of Nio's riveting and poignant journey. Much as a song can last with us forever attached to a memory or a moment, this book's rhythm and lyrics will grip your heart and provide motivation as you embrace and conquer life's challenges."

—**Jayson Yardley**
CEO
Knowtion Health

"I had the privilege of reading Nio's incredible book on overcoming trauma and finding joy. Through heartfelt storytelling and raw vulnerability, she shares deeply personal experiences of tragedy and adversity, yet manages to inspire and uplift with every page.

Nio's courage in sharing her journey serves as a symbol of hope for anyone facing their own struggles, showing that joy and fulfillment are always within reach, no matter the obstacles we encounter. Her words serve as a powerful reminder that life is indeed a precious gift, and how we choose to navigate its challenges ultimately defines our success.

I encourage anyone seeking inspiration, hope, and a reminder of the incredible resilience of the human spirit, to read this book. It's a testament to the power of perseverance and the beauty of finding joy amidst life's trials."

—**Debbie Jean Garrett**
MBA

JOY NOTES

"As a healthcare executive, I've encountered countless stories of resilience and triumph, but none have quite resonated with me like *Joy Notes* by Niobis Queiro. Through her captivating storytelling, Niobis shares her remarkable journey through trauma, triumph, and ultimate victory. Her ability to weave personal experiences into a tapestry of inspiration is truly remarkable.

Joy Notes isn't just a book; it's a roadmap for finding resilience and purpose in life's challenges. Niobis Queiro's words are not only empowering, but also deeply transformative. As a leader navigating the complexities of the healthcare industry, *Joy Notes* has been a beacon of encouragement for me, reminding me to embrace adversity and find joy in every step of the journey.

I highly recommend *Joy Notes* to anyone seeking inspiration, guidance, and a renewed sense of purpose. Niobis Queiro's wisdom is a gift to us all, and her book is a must-read for those striving to master their Zenith and lead with resilience."

—**Walter B. Davis**
President and CEO
Nevada Health Centers

"*Joy Notes* is a fantastic set of stories, weaving together a variety of the powerful experiences and remarkable people that shaped the course of a very accomplished woman's life. Nio has helped me navigate several very large life and career decisions over the course of our friendship, and reading these memoirs allowed me to better connect with the life experiences that have, in some part, now shaped me and those closest to me. This book surfaces strong truths about the difficulties and challenges faced in life, but it also provides a great opportunity for self-reflection and clarity."

—**Bradley Gallaher**
Co-founder, President, & Chief Strategy Officer
Switchboard, MD

DEDICATION

For my Mother, Niobis Mireya Cabrera Queiro, *Siempre Resiliente Sosteniendo Gozo y Amor.*

To the memory of:

- My Father, Antonio Queiro (1936 -2022), A Magical Force – Forever Present; and
- My Brother, Rafael Antonio Queiro (1960 – 2022), An Artistic Genius.

For my Husband Bob, and my son Quinton, my daughter-in-law Michelle, and my beacon of light, my grandson Cylas.

For my brother Henry, Man of God, and example to our youth.

For my nephews: Ulysses, Kyle, Joshua, and Cameron.

In more ways than one, they are part owners of my story.

ACKNOWLEDGMENTS

*J*oy! God's secret weapon to all believers. Without my faith in God, I would not be here to tell my story. Joy is an essential for the refreshment of the soul. I am grateful to the Lord for letting me find my joy and for leading me to share it with others.

"Count it all JOY, my brothers, when you meet trials of various kinds," says *James 1:2*.

Writing a book is a journey that encompasses the support of many who selflessly lift you up through the process when you have moments of doubt, insecurity, and self-criticism. I want to extend my infinite gratitude to the following amazing individuals:

Elizabeth Ann Atkins, author, publisher, and co-founder of Two Sisters Writing & Publishing®, thank you for your gentle guidance, acknowledgement, and validation throughout the process. This is would not be without you.

Walter B. Davis: President/CEO at Nevada Health Centers, Inc., thank you for being the first to tell me that my story needed to be told and for encouraging me to fulfill my purpose when it was not even clear to me.

Lora Carr, VP of Growth and Development for Accuity Healthcare, thank you for being my present angel when I was at my lowest. You help me find my way back with authentic joy and kindness.

JOY NOTES

Ramona Hernandez, servant leader, VP of Revenue Cycle at Knowtion Health, thank you, my dear spiritual sister. We sustain each other through joy and pain, grounded in respect and love.

Julie Shaw Noel, entrepreneur, honoring leader, woman of God, VP of Client Development at Cloudmed, thank you for being my sage mentor; I aspire to be the example of God's grace that you are. You see in me what most don't, and so I appreciate your honesty and support. You make me a better person.

Jayson Yardley, CEO of Knowtion Health, thank you for the continuous sponsorship and mentorship. You have been my advocate as a speaker and author. Your guidance has set my path to success; I am forever grateful.

Herman Williams, MD, thank you for sharing your story and journey with me. You helped me transform into life past the health crisis. Thank you for introducing me to Two Sister Writing & Publishing®.

Tufts Medical Center: thank you to the talented surgeons at Tufts Medical Center who saved both my and my husband's lives in 2021. Without you, none of this would have been possible. We honor: Dr. Tarnoff, Dr. Johnson, Dr. Chin, and Dr. Bugaev.

FOREWORD

This book is important because people need to be encouraged. People need to be uplifted. People need to be empowered and they need to see that they're not the only ones. They need to see that others have accomplished this. They need to see that these are ordinary people. Not rich people or well-known people, or well-situated people, just people.

When Nio asked me to provide the Foreword for *Joy Notes: Balancing the Trauma with Triumph,* I told her:

"Just know that this is what God is calling you to do. He is not calling you to do anything frivolous, or is going to take up your time just for the fun of it. He's going to use this and He'll use it mightily. I've often said that I stand in awe of a God who gives you gifts of talent and abilities with which to bless other people.

"And as you're doing it, you are being more blessed than they are. You can be God-given. Everything you do for Him, He gives back to you. He's just so awesome, so incredible, and yeah. I love the Lord."

This is my message for everyone reading this book as well. God has a calling for you, and perhaps this book can help you discover your calling, by finding your joy in music.

My joy and my calling truly have been song, and especially, "I Will Survive." I've traveled to more than 90 countries with this song.

My mantra is "I Will Survive," and it's because the song has become a core of my purpose: to give, to use that song to bring hope and encouragement to people from every walk of life, every race, creed, color, nationality, and age group.

And it's so fitting because, as I often say in interviews, Disco music—contrary to what people think—is the only music in the history of music ever to be . . . adopted by people from every race, creed, color, nationality, and age group.

No other music has done that, no matter how great the music is. It has with this particular audience. But this Disco music, everybody likes Disco music, and this particular song.

"I Will Survive" is a major theme in my life, literally. In fact, my story resonates with the mission of Nio's book, which explores how music was the saving grace for herself and other women during life-threatening health crises. You can read my health survival story in the last chapter of this book. Amazingly, God restored and elevated me immediately after my health crisis, by blessing me with this song in 1978.

["I Will Survive"—considered the women's anthem for empowerment—has had global success and was ranked by *Billboard* magazine among the "500 Best Pop Songs of All Time."]

After surviving a terrifying and sudden onset of paralysis, I left the hospital, fully convinced that God was going to do something; I just didn't know what.

I believed this, even when the record company sent me a letter saying that they were not going to renew my contract . . . which was up in a couple of months. So now I'm like, *Oh, my God, what am I going to do?*

I had been praying before, while I was in the hospital, and reading the Bible and all of that. I look back and can say I was half-hearted, because I didn't know of the Lord at the time. I had given my heart to the Lord when I was 16 years old and told my mother I wanted to be baptized, but then I forgot about it.

FOREWORD

Praise God, He didn't.

So, after the record company sent me that letter, of course, my faith in Him got more intense. Finally, they called me and said that they were going to renew my contract because they had gotten a new president over in England, where I was popular. And the record company got a hit with a song over there with the group called Cloud and they wanted to make sure it was a hit here in the United States. They didn't just import the record; they wanted me to record it. I hated the song, but I didn't care. I just wanted to keep my contract going.

They set me up in California to record the song [it was called "Substitute"]. And when I got out there, I asked, "What's going to be the B-side?"

They didn't know and asked what kind of songs I liked.

"I like songs that are meaningful and thoughtful, and touch people's hearts with melodies," I said.

"You know," they said, "we think you're the one we've been waiting for to record this song we wrote two years ago."

"Okay," I said. "What song is that?"

They wrote down the words for me.

[The song was written by Freddie Perren and Dino Fekaris, and it's about a woman finding her personal power after a terrible break-up.]

And I'm reading the words, and I'm like, "What are you, stupid? Do you want to put this on the B-side?"

And I'm sitting there, relating my spine surgery to the song, hoping I survive that. I'm thinking about the fact that my mother just passed away a few years ago, something I never thought I'd survive. I'm relating my life to the song, and I'm thinking, *Everybody who hears this song is going to do that.*

They say, "Well, it's staying on the B-side."

So, we recorded it and took it back to the record company. They wouldn't even listen to it. They put it on the B-side and put it out. When I got copies of it, I took it to Studio 54 [the famous Disco nightclub in New York City] to a really popular DJ there. I asked him to play it for the audience. They played it and the audience stormed the dance floor. Okay, I knew I was right about this because New York is so jaded, they don't immediately like anything.

This was different for me. So, I gave him the whole box [of records].

"Give the record to your DJ friends around New York," I said. "Let them play it for their audiences and let's see how that goes."

Of course, people began to request it. Then people began to call the radio station, because they wanted to hear it on the way home from work while they were in traffic. So, the record company started getting messages from the radio station, asking for the song. Anyway, our record company had to say, with much chagrin, "It's on the B-side!"

So, he started flipping it, and when they did a second release on it, they put it on the A-side. That is the story of "I Will Survive."

It's God's gift to me. As I say, it's a core of my purpose, and I use that song everywhere I go to uplift, encourage, and empower my audiences. It has become a family heirloom, with [mothers] passing it down to their daughters.

Now I hope that my story and the stories in Nio's book can help empower you and apply the lyrics of "I Will Survive" to any challenge you may be facing, because you *can* and you *will* survive.

— Gloria Gaynor
Grammy Award-Winning Artist
"I Will Survive"

CONTENTS

Dedication vii
Acknowledgments ix
Foreword xi
Introduction 1
Chapter 1 Nio's Story: Finding My Joy Notes 7
Chapter 2 Salsa: Finding Your Rhythm—
           My Father's Story 49
Chapter 3 The Blues—Out of Pain Comes Power 55
Chapter 4 Hip Hop—Misunderstood 69
Chapter 5 Soft Rock & Contemporary Christian Rebuilt .. 79
Photo Gallery 87
Chapter 6 Jazz—Improvise 91
Chapter 7 Country—Tell It Like It is,
           with Raw Honesty 107
Chapter 8 Rock 'n Roll: Embrace Your Wild Child 121
Chapter 9 Top 40—Shit Creek Survivor 145
Chapter 10 Disco Songstress Gloria Gaynor
           Says You Will Survive! 163
About the Author 171
Playlist 174
End Notes 175

INTRODUCTION

J.D. Salinger, the author of *Catcher in the Rye*, stated, "The fact is always obvious much too late, but the most singular difference between happiness and joy is that happiness is solid and joy is liquid."

Wiser words could not have been said. Striving for happiness is temporary satisfaction. Especially in this modern world where we live for instant gratification and temporary moments of happiness, and then what is next. We sit thinking of how to make ourselves happy again. This is an emotional rollercoaster can be endless.

Joy is different; it is full of gratitude, resiliency, purpose, consistency, selflessness, meaningful intention, and transformation. Joy is rooted in a spiritual nature that is centered on your core.

This book is my Joy journey through music as the vehicle of expression. Each note has a distinct sound when joined with others; you have a personal melody that sings your purpose, enabling perseverance through the cloudiest days.

I believe that music is the magical elixir in life, no matter how overwhelming the trauma, pain, or crises may be. Music—both listening to it, singing it, and playing it as a Classically trained pianist—has always soothed my mind, body, and soul. I have a song for every emotion, every occasion. It is a divine experience to immerse into the notes, the lyrics, voices, the symphonies of sound that sweep you into another dimension, far away from whatever is stealing your joy. With music, you are restored, healed, and lifted into a state of joy.

In this book, I'm sharing my story about how music continues to uplift and empower me. I also interviewed several dynamic women across America who share their stories about health crises and how music helped them heal. You'll also meet my husband, Bob, and hear his special relationship with music, and how songs help us to deeply bond and persevere through the most terrifying and life-threatening nightmares.

In our stories, you'll see how each person illustrates a particular musical genre and finds their *Joy Notes,* so you can do the same. Many of them embody many musical genres, because like lyrics and melodies, human beings are richly complex and multi-layered. Each note, chord, hook, bridge, instrument, and singing voice resonates with an emotion and an experience.

This book is about the harrowing things that women endure in healthcare and how we have our trauma, and we have to maneuver it through life because we're always moving forward. How did you move forward? What can you tell other women? And how did music empower you?

You know how a song gets in your head and you can't shake it? There are songs for a season that, when you hear them, provide a note of sage and peace. You are able to exhale, rejoice, dance, sway, and center yourself.

Music has been a part of my life since I was four years old. That's when I started to play the piano and fell in love with Classical music. I saw it as my little secret. None of my friends liked it or understood it, but for me, it was heaven. I would get lost in the complexity of the music and the stories of the

INTRODUCTION

composers. I remember playing Chopin and embracing the powerful quickness and difficulty of his piano pieces. At four years old, I had no idea that owning the rigor of practicing till my hands ached to learn to play Classical music was going to be a backdrop for my life. I found great joy in mastering the music and having it as my private delight.

What to expect in this book are stories that inspire you to own your joy. We will go through a musical journey that will empower you with sustainable tools to walk in joyful purpose. The music will empower you through the sorrow, invigorate you when tired. Make you lean your head back and close your eyes as it brings you back to peace and joy when you need it most. The power of using music as the force to carry on is life changing. Songs bring you to a place in time; you can smell the air and feel the raindrops or the warmth of the sun as you connect to the sounds, your body surrenders to the notes as you dance—sometimes in your head, chair, floor—it doesn't matter. It is your moment to own.

Music helped me release my tears and embrace the power of vulnerability and, like a phoenix, it swiftly led me to dry them and continue victoriously. The journey we are going to embark on in this book is my personal healthcare odyssey. It is an adventure that explores the good, bad, and ugly parts of healthcare, and how we can use our tragedies and trauma to find our voice and purpose.

This book also shares my story that begins in Cuba. They gave us one hour to pack everything my parents owned in one suitcase. This was our journey to America, and my personal story. I'm resilient. Resiliency happens when you step into the moment that you are having the trauma, and you realize that you need to breathe and accept the truth. You need to give yourself the space in the grace to understand that it's bad, and it's terrible. You're able to open your eyes, listen to some music, get your second breath, and then persevere. Whether it's a work-related challenge, whether it's a health challenge, you have to find your breath, then it's about being able to live. That is true resilience.

I also want you to understand that vulnerability is a secondary super hug. You see, when you hug vulnerability, you are relatable. You are that person who is willing to share of yourself. More importantly, you are able to let people into your space so that they can use it. Make it a point to be one. Stay curious and follow the prayers. I love the prayer that I have in my heart. I love what I do, but if I could start all over, I think I would have fallen into my purpose earlier. So now, I'm living with a purpose.

I want you to know that you cannot always survive your situation, but you can fly. I grew up with a woman who lives tormented in her traumas. She speaks of them as if they are happening again and again. No matter what I say to my mother, she just can't move past them. So, people will say, "But she's being resilient. She's done this; she's done that." No, she's still captive in her brain on those traumas. I really believe that a lot of the anger that we see in people, a lot of the toughness and grit that doesn't make sense, is deeply rooted in people who are trapped in a trauma.

Unfortunately, we as women stay in secrecy and pain.

We need a way to hug ourselves and not feel as though we are worthless. That we don't have the ability to be the best cheerleader for ourselves. We seem to always be seeking someone else to cheer for ourselves. We are our best cheerleader. We have the ability to find our strength. Your fate supports you. You have to make the determination that you'll be your best cheerleader. That's why I feel called to help women do this.

You don't survive three cardiac arrests because you don't have a purpose.

That's why this book is truly about just letting women

INTRODUCTION

who do everything for everyone else know that they can do something for themselves. And that's to free themselves. They can use the trauma as an open door to walk to the other side of their journey to find the beautiful symphony that life can become. That's what this book is: a guide to helping women find their joy notes. Those musical notes in your heart that can—no matter what's happening in your life—play a song that releases you from pain and helps you soar into a play of joy.

I'm wishing that for you. So please enjoy the stories from me and the phenomenal women I interviewed, and apply their words of wisdom to help you find your *Joy Notes*.

— **Niobis Queiro**
Author & Motivational Speaker

INTRODUCTION

who do everything for everyone else know that they can do something for themselves. And that's to free themselves. They can use the trauma as an open door to walk to the other side of their journey to find the beautiful symphony that life can become. That's what this book is: a guide to helping women find their joy notes. Those musical notes in your heart that can—no matter what's happening in your life—play a song that releases you from pain and helps you soar into a play of joy.

I'm wishing that for you. So please enjoy the stories from me and the phenomenal women I interviewed, and apply their words of wisdom to help you find your *Joy Notes*.

— **Niobis Queiro**
Author & Motivational Speaker

CHAPTER 1

Nio's Story: Finding My Joy Notes

My story starts in Cuba. I am the youngest of three born in Havana. I'm a daddy's girl, and was blessed with an incredible father. My dad is Tony, a man who lived a life based upon doing whatever he could to make a positive impact on others, no matter what the cost was to himself. He filled his wife's and children's lives with music, dance, and the arts. Tony had a bigger-than-life personality that made all he met feel loved and inspired to live abundantly. He was always able to bring fun to every moment, whether he was dancing salsa, working his design artistry, or putting aside his own needs to serve others. Everything was done in joy through music.

Tony liked to say that, during moments of adversity, "We should move forward with fearless intention." I first remember him telling the story of how he met Mireya (my mom) in Santiago de Cuba at a family party. He was taken by her and made the decision to pursue her, even though she had 10 brothers and a very strict father. It was the smile and tiny waist, and her guitar-shaped, slim body, that made him swoon.

So, with brazen courage, he showed up to the porch across the street from her house every day to listen to music and stare at her like a lost puppy. She and her sister did not know who the cute guy was interested in, but they knew he was handsome and dapper. Finally, one day, another guy started a conversation with Mireya, and he was not letting him get his girl. So, he knocked at her house and asked her father if he could get to know his daughter. His charm got a yes from her father and that started the beginning of the Queiro family.

But, not so fast. Soon after they started getting to know each other, Mireya got a scholarship to go to school in Havana, and she was gone from his life. He was completely crushed. He had friends in Havana and decided that he needed to go get his girl.

Tony was only 18 years old when he got to Havana and started a construction and upholstery business. He was so creative that he was in high demand. Tony knocked on the door of Mireya's brother's house and, this time, he went to ask for her hand in marriage.

Again, that charm and can-do spirit got him the beautiful Mireya. Years later, they were a happy couple with three kids, until an accident left Tony with a partial loss of vision. Not scared, together Mireya and Tony found a distant relative to sponsor them to come to America for surgery. In February of 1970, the family arrived in New York. Tony went to New York Eye and Ear Hospital for eye transplant surgery, but unfortunately, it failed.

When told he was eligible for permanent disability, he said, "No, I take care of my family." **He would tape his eye and go off to a factory to earn money to provide for his family.** In time, he moved on to work at Palisades General Hospital for 30 years, and kept a business designing incredible events and decorations. My dad worked day and night, six days a week, but Sundays were for his family. He would get up early and play his LPs of Classical and Cuban music while ironing our clothes to perfection. He loved to iron and make a crisp seam on his pants. The house was full of sounds, from Jazz, Ave Maria, Classical, and hip-shaking salsa. He loved it all.

When we were dressed and ready for church, he would have a magnificent breakfast on the table with amazing flower arrangements that he created, along with our best China, glasses, and cutlery. It was like being in a fine dining establishment. He wanted to make sure that we knew how to handle any situation. The music was the special touch. He taught me how to waltz, salsa, Cha-Cha, merengue and appreciate Classical music.

Once in America, I started to play piano with Isabel Zugaray, an incredible artist who made it so magical. Isabel always emphasized how music can enlighten moments, bring safety in despair, challenged me to persevere, channel strength, and celebrate my joy. Hence, the love of music was planted. I was addicted to the music. There was a radio show that was focused on teaching Classical music to children on WQXR in New York City. It was my favorite show. I was on pins and needles till 1:00 PM on Saturdays. I remember friends and family being shocked that I could identify the composers and the names of the songs. Music was in my soul.

That was a gift that made the difference several years later. At the age of eight, my mom and I went to her doctor for her annual OB/GYN visit. I was her translator. They found several lumps on her breast and I had to let her know the seriousness of the matter and the path ahead. She was so strong. She stayed quiet and then kissed my forehead, grabbed my hand, and took me to get ice cream. She loves ice cream. She never spoke about it with me. We would go to appointments, and she would try to find interpreters amongst the people in the waiting room or hospital. It was a hit or miss. On the no-assistance days, I was on deck as the translator.

I didn't know how to feel, as she was safeguarding me by showing no emotions. I started to believe that it was normal to live in and out of hospitals as a child, waiting in cold waiting rooms, doing my homework while she was going through treatment. I had a photocopy of a keyboard that I would use to practice my scales and songs when I was done with my homework. People would stare as they saw me touch the paper, as if we all could hear the notes. How I would get angry when I made a mistake and happy when it sounded perfect in my head. I was free in those moments.

Back then, there were no translators. Kids were it. Since I was inseparable from my mom, I went through the journey with her. There were two surgeries and lots of unexpected mishaps, but she came through. I learned how to keep a song in my heart through it all, as I went to a Spanish-speaking church, it was "Gozo en mi Alma" ("Joy in my Heart"). I woke up to that song. When concerned or confused, it ran through my thoughts and it calmingly put me to sleep.

This is also when I became determined to go into healthcare. I did not like that patients were not seen through their care journey or healing; it was all about treatment without communication or empathy. No one cared about the impact on the families or the financial strain, it just was not discussed. The bills were high and all I saw was my dad and mom work and work with not a word of complaint. She hid it all, the pain, stress, exhaustion, and tears. There were no babysitters or extended family to support us, only strong God-cored, resilient parents.

Everyone lived in a web of secrecy in regard to illness. During that era, the prevailing medical establishment's attitude was that it was the patient's fault for getting sick. I was perplexed about that as a child, but I knew I was going to do something about it in the future. I found the **Joy Note of passion in C major.** Of course, I loved the group Journey

CHAPTER 1

during this time, and their song that became the anthem of the downtrodden, "Don't Stop Believin'." Passion can make that which does not seem possible obtainable. It cuts through the pain and is beside you through the victory and beyond. Finding your passion is not limited by age and circumstances during the bleakest times. Passion has a breath and beat to move forward with.

When I was 10, my mom took ill again, but this was different. We were at church. It was Sunday. We had just finished Sunday school and were going into the main sanctuary, but my mom looked gray. She started throwing up blood. It was the scariest moment. It looked like a horror movie. It all became slow motion as she was convulsing and hurling blood everywhere as we stood in the doorway by the exit of the Sunday school rooms. It was a small, tight space with a red curtain as the divider that matched the pool of blood on the cream tiles.

My middle brother, Henry, and I were calm, just rubbing her back, and I saw my oldest brother, Ralph, run to get a bucket. I don't know how he knew where to go. So many people were screaming, but not helping. The pastor moved the people away and tried managing the situation. The screaming stopped and the noise settled as people started leaving, as they were asked to. Only the pastor, the youth pastor, and Carmen, my mom's best friend, remained.

My mom was frail and disoriented. All we wanted to do as her kids was to safeguard her. We moved to the parent role in this situation. Childhood was completely lost as we knew it. The silence of the room was suffocating. This was church, where the music flowed and healed all wounds. This was a safe place. But at this moment, it was a quiet room with my mom lying on chairs as a makeshift bed, wet by her blood, vomit, and lifelessness. Then prayers overtook the room. The prayers somehow became rhythmic and soothing. Then, out of nowhere, the ambulance crew came in and asked us to move away. She lost consciousness at that point, my mom's best friend, Carmen, swooped us up, and the next thing I knew, she was gone to the hospital.

We stayed at the church for a while. I remember running to the piano and playing Beethoven's "Fur Elise" repeatedly. It calmed me down till we left for the hospital and caught up with my dad. She had a large ulcer that had ruptured. They had to remove several feet of her intestine. She was in Christ Hospital in Jersey City, New Jersey, for more than three months; some of that time she was in a coma.

My brothers and I would ride our bikes four miles to the hospital from West New York, New Jersey, and sneak into her room, as kids under 13 were not allowed to visit. We would go through central receiving, past the morgue, and take the stairs to her room. The nurses were kind and acted as if we were invisible to let us visit.

I would sit there and tell her about my day, read to her, and sing her favorite church hymns to her. My brother, Henry, and I managed the household during this period of time. My dad worked harder than ever. We had the "latch key kid" routine down packed. Henry would write the checks for the bills and help me with the laundry, and I kept the house tidy. My dad would pay a barrio restaurant to supply us a cantina that gave us a daily three-course meal. Breakfast we made for ourselves, and lunch was at school. Yes, we were kids who truly needed that school lunch, and yes, we paid for it, too. Most importantly, our life was a secret. We did not share with others what we were going through as kids. To the outside world, we were normal. I learned how to shop to keep myself looking immaculate.

My mom was in and out of the hospital for the next three years. There were more surgeries and bouts of Dumping Syndrome, an illness that makes the stomach empty too fast,

CHAPTER 1

causing nausea, diarrhea, dizziness, and other problems. The music grew in me and gave me space to breathe and feel normal. Piano and dance twice a week required two hours of practice daily. I did everything to make my parents proud and not to worry about me.

Yes, these were very traumatic years. At home, I wanted to be invisible, except for making sure they were proud and happy. When I had my piano and dance recitals on stage, I was alive. Like all the other girls, I had smiles surrounding me and music guiding me. I remember all the recitals and piano competitions.

When I was 12, I had a special year. Not only did I score the highest in my age category for piano, but I had my first dance solo. I remember standing out from the dance chorus line and spinning like a top with great precision. The crowd cheered, the cameras were flashing, and a standing ovation followed. Through these years, I found my *Joy Note* of **Self-Worth in A minor.** I am worthy as I am, so I do walk in JOY. Queen's song, "We Are the Champions," rang in me. I told myself, *I can make it happen and I will look forward to the finish line. Only I can stop myself from success.* I understood that I needed to be my own cheerleader. *Others' words and negativity will never hurt me because that is not my truth.*

We had some good years during high school and my first few years of college. I met my first husband during freshman year during the sorority rush season. My roommate asked me to go on a double date with her, but she and I were going to her date's cousin's bar. I had never been to a bar. I was a 16-year-old sheltered virgin—I was so nervous and curious at the same time. So, off we go, and as soon as we get to the bar, the owner came up to us and said, "Get that child out of here now." My friends all stared at me and we piled back in the car and went to McDonald's.

That day, I met my husband, Maurice Anthony (everyone called him Tony). He was quiet, kind, tall, and handsome. He wanted to make it up to me that we could not get into the bar. So he got me a fake ID. It was hilarious. He took a picture of me, and three days later, I had a New Jersey driver's license. It was special and fun.

We dated, and during the summer of my sophomore year, he proposed by filling my summer apartment with red paper hearts and balloons from the ceiling, while the floor was covered with rose petals. He was on one knee when I arrived. Of course, I said yes. We planned for the wedding to be during the summer of my junior year, as he was graduating first that summer and I would follow the next year. He had to promise my parents that I would finish my education and live my life dreams.

Two months post-proposal, he made a decision that took the plan in a different direction. He dropped out of school and signed up for the Navy. He had gotten terrible grades in the first semester of senior year and decided he was not happy with the fact he would not be able to graduate on time or support us after marriage. I was lost and furious. I thought of breaking it off, but I hated that it would mean that my parents and brothers were right, that he was not the right match for me. We continued with the wedding plans as he went off to basic training in Chicago. We wrote each other weekly and found an elevated relationship through letters.

I decided to focus my energy on music. I was going to New York and playing back music and singing for recording studios. This is where I was at my best, and I let my mom and dad plan the wedding.

You can't ignore your life as much as you want to run away from the drama. I was in my dorm room and I had a sharp pain in my left eye; it was indescribable. I couldn't see out of that eye at all. It was dark and I was having a migraine. I remember getting dressed and following my known steps to my car. I was using memory to guide me home. To this day, I

CHAPTER 1

don't know how I made it to West New York from Union, New Jersey, without having an accident. By the time I got home, I could not get my key in the door, so I pressed the doorbell.

My mom came to the door and screamed. What I did not know was that my eye was out of my socket and my face was swollen beyond recognition. My mom and dad brought me inside and I lost consciousness. When I woke up, my mom was placing warm chamomile compresses on my face, and soon after, a doctor was at my bedside. He was an ophthalmologist friend of the family who kindly made a house call. The value of a small, tight-knit Cuban community paid off.

He said that it looked as if I had a tumor. Guess where he sent me? To the same hospital where my dad had been admitted when we arrived in the United States. There, two months prior to my wedding, I was partially blind. I had an emergency appointment. When I arrived, my mom guided me, as my eyes were swollen and I had little to no sight. All my senses were heightened, my hearing was on high alert, and every step was a sensitive pressure of weight distribution. I was taken to a room that they used to do ultrasounds of the eye. It was so cold in there; I was wearing a sundress, as it was August in New York. The room smelled like Clorox and alcohol, and there was little furniture except for a table that I bumped my foot against, a chair with no arms that my mom led me to, and the ultrasound machine.

Mom stood next to me, rubbing my shoulders as we waited. It was strange to see her so worried. I was perplexed. She never showed that level of emotion. *I'm causing unnecessary stress for her,* I thought, *I have to heal quickly. Yes, that's the plan.* Finally, the young tech came into the room. I would not be able to pick her out of a lineup, as she was a mere blurred figure to me. She couldn't get an image due to all of the swelling and because my eyelid was not opening. She ran out of the room and a tall male figure with a deep voice told me that he was going to give me a shot in my eye. Due to all the swelling, I felt nothing but dizziness and confusion. Five doctors circled me in a matter of minutes.

Later, I was made aware that one medical chief and four residents were tending to me. The diagnosis was a Pseudotumor cerebri, also called idiopathic intracranial hypertension. The intracranial pressure causes swelling of the optic nerve and results in vision loss. There is no obvious reason for this to occur. I was given medication to reduce the swelling and I wore an eye patch. I was able to get enough vision back to see from my right eye to return to school and work as a tutor. I remember going home for pre-wedding planning, and my dad had covered an eye patch in white satin and pearls that matched my dress. It made me cry and laugh, thinking, *Not even blindness gets me out of this wedding.*

By the time of the wedding, my swelling had diminished enough that all I had was a lovely moon face from the large amounts of Prednisone that I was taking on a daily basis. My vision was still a challenge, but I learned to live with it. It would take three more months before I was back to normal sight.

On a hot day in August, we married. It was a fairytale wedding with a horse-drawn carriage and more than 200 attendees for our sit-down, candlelit dinner. The next day, I was in Virginia Beach where Tony was stationed. We had a brief honeymoon there, as he had limited leave time available. We did all the things that newlyweds do for five days, and then I got on a plane and returned to my senior year at college. We went back to weekly letters. He'd come visit when he could, if he was not deployed. This went on for a year till graduation.

The week after graduation, my friend, Marta Martinez, got in my blue Monza and we started our *Thelma and Louis* journey to military housing in Little Creek Naval Base in

CHAPTER 1

Virginia Beach, Virginia. Of course, this was minus Brad Pitt and a dual suicide.

Marta and I drove the seven-hour trip in 10 hours. Of course, my wonderful Monza broke down, even though a tune-up and oil change were done prior to the trip. It was a Monza, one of the worst cars made by Chevy. Muscle car light, they called it. I called it "leave me on the side of the road" reliability. My radiator sprung a leak. We were adding fluid every 15 miles, barely making it through the 17.6 miles of the Chesapeake Bay Bridge Tunnel. We never stressed. We knew what to do, and every time we stopped, someone would show up to help. From the hippie van, to Grandpa and Grandma, we met the nicest people. We took the adversity in stride and embraced all the new acquaintances we made as guiding angels.

Finally, we made it to my new home, a small one-bedroom, one-bath townhome in Virginia Beach. It was quaint (small) and had all the essentials. When we arrived, the neighbors were outdoors and quickly came over and introduced themselves. Marta and I were awestruck, as we were from Jersey, where people mind their own business and speak to no one. Here was all this Southern/military hospitality. I was quickly made aware of the dos and don'ts of being a military wife.

I entered a new phase in my life, as I captured a new note of joy: **Gratitude in F sharp Major.** Relationships are key in life, as Dionne Warwick sings in "That's What Friends Are For." I was also learning how to be a good relationship partner, which is a major skill in life. The balance of give and take, honesty, and kindness, while standing in the gap, pushing the little bird off the nest to fly, and dancing to a mutually loved song—priceless!!

In September, I sat for my Registered Health Information Administrator (RHIA) test and passed with flying colors. Now, I could get a job. I was in need, as the Monza was in a crash that my husband survived without a scratch, but the car was destroyed. I needed a new car. I started the interview process.

I was very excited about my interview at Hampton General Hospital. The job was a starter coding position. Being a military wife, there was a great deal of pushback on hiring for leadership positions, as deployment could happen unexpectedly. So, I was playing it safe. The interview with Tom went well—so well that I went to the car dealership and started test driving cars. I finally found the one, and I sat in the dealership, excited about the prospect of getting a new Hyundai Excel GLS, new on the market at that time. My first manual drive, zippy little car. But there was a problem. How was I going to pay for this beauty?

My dealer asked me that same question as I sat there in a daze. I asked him for a phone book. I looked up the florist near Hampton Hospital. I called the first one and made an order for a dozen white roses to be sent to Tom, thanking him for the opportunity to be a new member of the medical records coding team. I asked the florist to let me know when it got delivered. I gave them the dealership's number, as I was not leaving without my new car. Two hours later, the call came in. By then, I had ordered and enjoyed a pizza with the sales team. I also tag-teamed and made a sale of another Excel. I became part of the team. Once I got the all-clear from the florist, I was ready to give Tom a call. My newfound mates hovered around me as I picked up the phone and dialed his number. He answered the phone on the second ring (oh, the anticipation) and when he heard my voice, he said, "You are a go-getter. I've never gotten flowers from an interviewee."

My response was, "I believe that if you truly want something, you need to stand out from the pack."

He said, "You have the job."

I then had to ask how much it paid. He said $3,000 less than what I needed to get my car. I took a deep breath and

CHAPTER 1

asked for $4K more. I explained that I needed to be able to purchase a car for transport to and from the job safely. We laughed.

"You have gumption!" he said. "Yes, that is within range of the position."

The sales team roared. I apologized for the background noise.

"Are you at the car dealership?"

"Yes, I am."

I asked for a fax stating that I got the job and the salary. The fax came minutes later as a handwritten note on hospital stationery. I left the dealership in my silver Excel GLS. As the radio was blasting, **"I am Woman, Hear Me Roar"** by Helen Reddy, I drove away.

Tom was an amazing boss who believed in me. He introduced me to the Chief Financial Officer of a small community hospital where I started my first management role. He was a great man and mentor. We lost him way too fast. I learned a new *Joy Note* from Tom: **Never Settle in the key of E minor.**

You are deserving of the best, and settling to be safe is like wearing sneakers to every occasion. Sure, you are comfortable, but never have a polished, complete look. You're just living without enjoying your full potential. I know someone is going to say, "What is wrong with just being comfortable?"

If it's so great, then why do the ladies who live in comfortable shoes and clothes often provide unsolicited excuses and apologies regarding their appearance? Because they know that they're settling instead of taking a calculated risk on themselves. You're an example, and if you want your children to soar, you must take risks, fail, and get back up on your feet gracefully, ready to try again with your new-found knowledge.

As a Cuban woman in my GenX generation, you married early and you had kids right away. I was no different than most of my friends—married at 19 and immediately working on a baby. Our first attempt occurred while I was still in my senior year of college. It seemed that if Tony looked at me, I got pregnant (that was the joke), but I was not able to cross the finish line with a healthy baby.

Our first miscarriage happened while I was pregnant with twin girls, well in my fifth month. I woke up from the pain and saw a pool of blood on my sheets. I called 911. The pain was relentless, and my tears were inconsolable. I was alone, living in a high-rise in Irvington, New Jersey. We had a studio apartment with a dressing room and a fabulous walk-in closet.

Tony was somewhere in the Atlantic Ocean in a submarine. I sat on our four-post bed in the middle, surrounded in blood, frozen. I felt cold and alone. I didn't want to call my parents, and Tony was not reachable. The bleeding would not stop, and I was getting weak. The elevator had broken around 3 PM, and I was on the tenth floor. By the time they reached me, it was too late. I had horrible cramps and I felt the urge to push. I screamed, held my knees back, and a tiny, wrinkled baby-form came out. It was one of two. The second left as if someone were scraping my insides raw. She was sideways. I manually repositioned her. It was an instinctive move to make the pain go away. She came out without tearing me up. My wedding bed turned into the death sheets of my little babies. I was tired, drenched in blood, and broken.

The door flew open. It was EMS. Two young men—one tall, the other average height—could not believe the scene. The tall one said, "Are you ok?"

No. He got closer and saw my babies and that the cord was attached. The other EMT cut the cord, all in an eerie silence, out of respect for the dead. I was dead myself, inside. *Why?*

I was admitted because I had lost so much blood with

a planned D&C in the morning. I could not imagine going through that alone, and I didn't. In the morning, my mom and dad were there, holding my hand as I continued to cry. I missed turning in an assignment that was essential for graduation. My husband arrived mid-day. The procedure was over, and I was calmer, but broken.

My husband asked, "What can I do?" I told him about my paper and that it was late. He ran home and took the folder to the professor, who was in office hours. He explained the situation to her. Her answer was, "Late is late." She failed me. Tony knew she would, but wouldn't tell me. I found out when I got back to school and checked the grade wall. I'd never failed a class in my life. *Why was this happening?* I ran to the dean's office with my paper in hand. It had a B crossed out and a D in red over it. I explained what had happened and he assured me that I would graduate.

I learned so much about life. You can't control people, as they come with all forms of anger and individuality. I had met cruel people before, but this was anger and attitude that transcended understanding. I could not control any aspect of life then. All I had was my faith and the musical notes that assured me that my passion, self-worth, relationships, and never-settle spirit would guide me to move forward. Control is not a positive trait.

The lesson I found in this was, embrace your **vulnerabilities,** and the song that expresses this is, **"What's Going On" by Marvin Gaye.**

Shortly after, there was another miscarriage, this one within the first trimester, and we told no one. Now, I was living with Tony and working at Hampton General Hospital. Our life was solid and we thought, *Why not try again?* I charted my menstrual cycle and checked my temperature. Ahh, the wonderful rhythm system. We needed a plan, a healthy diet. I was working out. I was going to make this time count.

JOY NOTES

October 31st, 1986, I got pregnant 30 days to the day of our plan. It was our secret. I saw the best OB/GYN in Hampton, Virginia. I was high-risk, so even though we lived in Virginia Beach, I would stay at a hotel close to the hospital if I was not feeling well. Otherwise, I was home with Tony, craving Church's Chicken and Dairy Queen (don't judge me). The two were across town from each other and Tony was willing and able to take the trek to satisfy my craving. By the time he returned, I was bleeding like a river. He picked me up in his arms and took me to the ER at Sentara in Norfolk. I was losing my babies. I was devastated. I remember the nurse, a slim middle-aged, tall blonde woman, asking me:

"Do you know who the father is?" She did not make any eye contact or acknowledge me as an individual.

I responded with tears streaming down my face, "My husband is parking the car."

Her response was, "Uhmm, right." Her attitude was as sterile as the white room, void of any character, and her next statement was an order: "Give me your Medicaid card." I can hear her voice clearly in my head and see the sour look of judgment across her face.

"I'm married and my husband is parking the car," I said. "And I have BCBS insurance. I work at a hospital." Then I shared my history, but as I was in mid-sentence, she walked out of the room.

When she returned, Tony was in the room holding my hand.

"I guess you are the father," she said. "She sure can't hold those babies in till her due date, can she? You got a defective one there."

I was crushed and demoralized all in one fast moment. The worst thing was the lack of eye contact. It was as if I were invisible. A dog receives more respect than I did in that ER.

I never saw a doctor, just a nurse. She opened her mouth once more and said, "We will do a D&C shortly. No need to

CHAPTER 1

waste time on this. We will get things set up. "Tony lifted me up in his arms and walked us back to the car and drove like a bat out of hell to Hampton General Hospital. We arrived at the ER and the experience was completely different. The OB team came down and immediately, IVs were placed, my doctor was called, and we found out that I had lost one of the twins through an ultrasound, but that the remaining baby had a strong heartbeat. Hence, I had a procedure to save the remaining fetus and a transabdominal Cerclage was installed. From then on, I was on bed rest. I stayed in the hospital for several weeks.

Having nothing else to do, I asked Tom, "Are we falling behind on coding and can I do some coding of charts?" A cart was brought up daily and I happily coded the day away. I guess I was a remote worker ahead of my time.

July finally came and I was steady and healthy. We counted the hours and the days. Quinton was due on July 26th. On the 25th, the hospital was having a picnic. I begged Tony for us to go, so I could get out of the house and be close to the hospital if the time came (that was my story and I'm sticking to it—in reality, I was bored).

We went to the hospital picnic and they were playing softball. I wanted to be a part of the fun. I knew I could bat well, so I requested to come in as a pinch hitter. Of course, the guys laughed—until I hit the ball hard and far over their arms, head deep into the outfield. I was planning just to walk the bases, but someone picked up the ball and was running to third base to call me out. I started to run, and I could hear the crowd telling me, no stop running, but my competitive nature kept me going. I slid into third base, and as I slid in, so did the contractions, starting fast and furious.

"Labor!" I yelled.

It was hilarious to see some of the medical staff running the opposite way to get away from the liability, but the faithful nurses came to me and helped me up. My husband appeared like Flash Gordon and picked me up, and off to the car we went. Everyone started packing up, and just like that, we had a caravan to the hospital—eight cars beeping and running lights to get through the five miles to the hospital. The energy was infectiously high and full of excitement. The baby was coming.

It took 36 hours for Quinton to see this wonderful world, as he wanted to make sure that he arrived on his actual due date. To this date, this is a man who is always mindful of being on time. His birth was a beautiful moment in my life. I was given the responsibility to guide a life and provide good core values. He was born in a birthing bed in a cold OR room at Hampton General. My doctor, Dr. Curtis, was in shorts and a tank shirt, having come off his boat to deliver my prince. The energy was high in the room, with great laughter about music. Soft Rock played in the labor room. I was very stubborn and refused to scream, instead just following instructions to push.

One of the nurses came over, since progress was slow, and said to me, "It is okay to not be in control. Nobody is here to judge. Relax and the baby will relax."

I exhaled and cried all at the same time, and Quinton came into this world, a healthy seven-pound, 11-ounce, 21.5-inch boy. All was well with the world. I was in a wonderful, safe place.

During that ride to the hospital, I remembered the love, oneness, selflessness, and authenticity of the group. This was an **empathetic culture,** one that I not only cherished, but captured as a G major. The country song "Humble and Kind" played in my heart—it does every time I get exposed to a culture of belonging and kindness.

Some people would say that means you have to accept things that, based on my beliefs, are not godly. No. What it means is that you accept that we all come with talents that

CHAPTER 1

together make us unstoppable. My beliefs are what I practice in my life, but I do not force them on others and the Lord said not to judge. Judging stifles growth and creativity. It provides unnecessary pain. Respect and empathy provide an environment where all are accountable and responsible for their decisions and empowered to bring their best to the occasion.

Life continued with its ups and downs. I divorced and returned to New Jersey to be close to family and ensure my son had good role models, who included my dad and brothers. I was working at the Greater New York Hospital Association in my first consulting role, performing DRG validation services. At the same time, I was experiencing some serious changes in my body. I started gaining weight, yet my diet and exercise routine were the same. My shoe size had gotten larger; migraines were constant. My vision was failing me and I stopped having menstrual cycles (this one I was happy about, though I knew it was not a good thing).

I was turning 30 in a few days and I went to lunch with my mom. I told her what was going on and she said, "You need to see a doctor." What she did not know is that I had seen seven different doctors. The last one had said he believed that I had mental health issues, and essentially that I was a hypochondriac because my labs were negative and he could not find a cause.

"I can't take another doctor telling me my symptoms are not real," I told my mom.

She picked up the phone and scheduled me an appointment with her OB/GYN. She was most concerned of the lack of menstruation.

The appointment was on my birthday, a scandalous way to spend your birthday. The building was a two-story house on a beautiful tree-lined street in North Bergen, New Jersey. The brownstone stood out, as it was immaculate with a large front door. I opened the door and went to the left into the waiting room. It was empty. The receptionist greeted me and we quickly went through the intake paperwork, and I was ushered back to the exam room. The room was light and airy with wonderful landscape art. The table of Discomfort was in the center waiting for me. I disrobed and sat at the edge, wishing I were anywhere but there.

The doctor entered, and seemed different than the rest. He sat down and started having a conversation with me. He leaned in with interest, no interruptions. He asked questions with curiosity. I was being "seen" for the first time in a long time by a clinician. He then asked his nurse to join us. He explained that he wanted to do a full thyroid panel and wanted me to get a CAT scan. She took my blood and went off.

Later, I found out that the office was closed. I was given a special appointment. I went to Christ Hospital for my CAT scan. When I arrived, again, it was empty, but they took me immediately. The CAT scan was of the brain with contrast. I laid on the table and they placed a cage over my face. My heart started racing; I thought I was going to throw up or pee myself. I was hyperventilating.

"Please keep still," said the voice behind the glass. "Count to 10 or cue your favorite song in your head. Please calm down."

I started counting and following the breathing prompts. After what seemed like forever, it was over. The cage was off my face. The knocking noise from the machine stopped. I heard, "All done!" But nope, that was the beginning.

As I left the hospital, my cell phone started ringing. Back in the day, phone calls in the middle of the day were expensive and not a common practice. I recognized the number. It was the doctor's office. The voice on the other side said, "Can you please come back to the doctor's office? He'd like to talk to you." I started to say, "I have plans, it's my birthday."

CHAPTER 1

But I didn't. I drove to the office. Honestly, I was scared, as it was unusual to have a doctor call you after you have a series of tests.

When I opened the office door, this time it was packed with patients. I went to sit in the last empty chair and the nurse said, "Ms. Queiro, please come with me." I walked through a room full of angry pregnant women, glaring at me for cutting the line. I walked with an apologetic look on my face.

I was asked to go into the doctor's office. I sat in this expansive, mahogany-rich room full of custom bookcases, a large desk with a throne for a chair, plus two club chairs set in front of the desk. The wall with no bookcases displayed his diplomas and what seemed like hundreds of baby pictures. I sat in the club chair closest to the window and the large plant that flanked the corner. The room was cold and the wait was eternal, even though he entered within five minutes. Finally, there he was.

He did not go to his desk. He sat in the club chair next to me and looked me in the eyes. He looked sad as he sat there, and then he said, "I forgot to tell you 'Happy Birthday' when you were here earlier."

"I had to come back for that," I said. "Don't worry, it's not a big deal."

"No," he said, "we need to talk about your CAT scan preliminary results. The radiologist found that you have three tumors, and some cranial bleeding that we believe happened recently. The tumors vary from the size of a pinhead to the size of the inside of your ring. You have Pituitary Tumors. The good news is, they are generally benign, but we really don't know that at this point. The first course of treatment we will try is to shrink them with medication. If that does not work, we can explore a surgical course."

I sat there frozen, my brain only focused on my nine-year-old that I was charged to raise. I thought, *I have to complete this goal at all costs.* I shut down. He called my name two to three times before I acknowledged him.

"Thank you," I said, standing up.

"Wait, we are not done."

"Oh."

The doctor added, "I've sent a prescription to your pharmacy and I booked you with our neurologist for follow-up."

"Okay," I said.

Next, I started a special program with the great Dr. Bruce from New York Presbyterian. The meds had a violent effect on me. I would go into a seizure. I was not able to function at work or home. I had to go on FMLA—the Family and Medical Leave Act—a terrifying situation for the main provider of income and care for my small family. I was losing weight rapidly, as I could not hold food or liquids down. My diet consisted of ice chips. I could not focus in a room with any noise; everything had to be a whisper. The saddest part of it was seeing my son's eyes full of concern and fear for his mom. I knew that feeling. I knew the mental trauma and anguish of my nine-year-old. Here, history repeated itself; a child living through a parent declining in front of their eyes.

I would make sure that he had play dates, and was busy with sports and chess. We used to love to play chess together, but now I could not see the board well enough, nor concentrate to make good strategic moves. I made sure it wasn't a secret, and my family swooped in to help. I had to get better for him.

I changed neurologists twice. I was left hopeless, not knowing what was next. Then, my partner at the time talked to his boss and got a referral to Dr. Puglises of Hackensack, New Jersey. At this time, I could barely get out of bed, so he made a house call. I was in bed when this tall, thin, older man appeared in my sight. He introduced himself and said, "You were on my way home, so I thought it would be good to check on you. Do you have your films?"

CHAPTER 1

"Yes, sir, my previous doctors said I was to have them with me everywhere I went, in case something happened to me."

I had copies in my car, home, and desk at my job. There was no EMR (Electronic Medical Records) back then, only paper and films to carry. I also had copies of my full medical record. I would get copies of every office visit, as I often saw doctors in different hospitals. So many referrals and so many doctors who were merely treating the symptoms. No one spoke about a solution or a plan of action.

The quiet gentle giant who was Dr. Puglises was different. He was at my bedside holding my hand, telling me, "You are going to be fine, we are going to remove those tumors and get your life back."

I turned my head and looked at him in disbelief.

A week later, I was having PATs done, and I was scheduled for surgery that Friday at 6 AM. My mom and dad took me into the hospital. We met the surgery team, and everyone was very nice and reassuring that this was going to be an uneventful two-to-three-hour surgery.

Three hours into the surgery, Dr. Puglises came out to see my parents in a private room.

"We lost her for a full minute," he told them, "but she came back. She had a stroke and had brain hemorrhage during surgery. The next 48 hours are going to be delicate."

"Let me pray for you before you go back into surgery," my mom asked.

He complied, understanding that she wanted God to bless him as he worked on her baby girl, her youngest child.

During surgery, I woke up in another realm. I was hovering over my body, seeing the team in chaos. The Jazz music was turned off, and I saw a crash cart being brought in. I could see my limp body, but not my face. My leg and chest were fully exposed. A young blonde doctor came into the room and started working on my chest. It was rapid-fire and all I could feel was that I wanted it to stop and go away. I remember having a conversation in my head, with me saying:

"I want to rest, this is too much."

"This is not your time," the other voices said.

"Quinton," I said.

"This this is not your time," the voices repeated.

Everything went dark and I was under anesthesia again. The surgery continued and they removed three tumors and used some fat from my thigh to fill the space. (Now, when I look at the scar, I think of it as a scar of triumph.)

When I woke up in the PACU, there was Dr. Puglises sitting next to me. He looked so tired, still in scrubs, with a bonnet on his head. I looked up at him and he said, "Welcome back."

I tried to speak, but nothing came out. I wanted to thank the blonde Dr. Rosen, but I could not formulate words, just grunts. Someone brought a pad and a pencil. I wrote like a three-year-old: "Thank you all, blonde DR, too."

Dr. Puglises asked, "How do you know about Dr. Rosen?"

I shrugged.

I was moved to the ICU. I had trouble keeping my oxygen saturation levels stable. The stroke impacted my motor skill, speaking, and ambulatory steadiness. I was in the ICU for three weeks, and my mom never left my side. She slept in the waiting room outside of the ICU. The hospital would feed her, and after several days, they brought a cot into my room that was rolled away in the morning. I was so blessed to be at a hospital that knew I needed the family support to recover, and they were creative. Mom made sure never to be in their way when I had to be flipped, so I would not have sores, and she continuously asked questions of the Physical Therapy and Occupational Therapy techs, so I would be able to continue my training at home.

After a month in the hospital, I was finally discharged. I was taken to the Ear, Nose and Throat specialist who assisted

CHAPTER 1

in the surgery to remove my nasal packing. Since surgery was sphenoidal, the approach was through my nasal cavity. The removal of the packing was uncomfortable and it felt like you're in a magician's act. The ENT pulls packing tape for what seems like hours. You are told that you cannot sneeze or blow your nose for several weeks.

This made me visualize a totally unrealistic scenario of me sneezing in the middle of the night and my brain pouring out. My next stop was Kessler Rehab Hospital; the actor Christopher Reeves, who was paralyzed by a horse riding accident, was receiving his rehab at the same time. We were one floor apart. This was a very expensive place to get care. But they got it done incredibly well. However, they never saw Mireya Queiro coming. My mom believed that she could get me well faster. So, I went outpatient and tried her methods, along with the Kessler program.

The brain stayed in place—no sneeze fall-out. However, due to one tumor being on my optic nerve, I only regained vision in my left eye, blind forever on my right. My speech and motor skills came back. My mom being a genius, she did research and would push me in my chair to Queens, New York, on the train. The world is not disabled-friendly. Elevators often don't work and the gap between the trains and the landings are often uneven and hard to get a wheelchair on and off. My mom is a tiny lady, barely five feet, and had the strength of a sumo wrestler.

She created a therapy program that included acupuncture, cupping, an herbalist, and me practicing the piano an hour a day to get my hands agile again. We would walk up and down stairs and hills. My PT and OT therapist were amazed at my progress. I was ahead of the plan.

When I finally returned to meet with Dr. Puglises (four weeks post-discharge), I walked in without assistance. I was speaking at 70% accuracy. I found that when tired, I was not able to hold long conversations and my pronunciation became impaired. I walked into his office and he looked at me confused.

"I thought we were going to be discussing permanent disability planning," he said.

"Nope, I have too much to do," I said. "I have a child to raise."

He laughed without abandonment and said, "Let's plan to get you to meet your goals, Warrior Princess."

I had told him the story of Wonder Woman, and how my son brought me a figurine to the hospital and gave it to me to cheer me up. I was his Wonder Woman.

I returned to work four weeks later. It took two years to get used to my limited sight and new awkward body. I became an expert at masking my deficits and being able to not get people to notice the struggle below the façade of the well-dressed, polished woman they viewed.

Through it all, I learned **perseverance and resiliency. My mom was the example.** You may have noticed that I did not have friends coming to the rescue. I was not too surprised that my few friends did not come along for the ride. I was going through something that they could not imagine, and during our late twenties and early thirties, most are self-centered and do not know how to give openly. It was my journey, and I could not worry about others' support. I had the right people that I needed to make it through. I got stronger and wiser through this time, and I learned that each struggle was a teaching moment, and it moved forward and away from a past failure. The Wonder Woman theme song was my ringtone, and it drove me forward the key of G major.

I was blessed to see my son grow and blossom into a great young man. During his senior year in high school, I was driving alone to a Healthcare Financial Management Association event in New Jersey, where I was to be a speaker. A driver on the opposite side of the road fell asleep at the wheel and

CHAPTER 1

his car came directly at me, pinning me in between the car in front and behind me. My small BMW Z4 was a pretzel, all airbags deployed. I lost consciousness. The accident closed I-78. When I woke up, I noticed that I was trapped in the car; I couldn't feel my legs. I heard the EMS say, "I am not sure if she is breathing." I tried to blink. I did not even think of screaming. They used the jaws of life to get me out.

I was able to stand for a mere second before I plummeted to the ground. I was taken to a local hospital. I had a broken left leg and crushed right foot. I would not let them do the surgery there. I called my car service that I always used to get to and from the airport for business travel and asked them to pick me up. Next, I phoned my fiancé and told him to meet me at our community hospital. I called the chief of the orthopedic department and told him my story. He said, "See you in the ER." The car service came, they helped me into a wheelchair, and they set me on my back across the backseat of the Escalade. I was not to put any weight on my legs. As I got to the ER an hour later, they were ready for us. I went directly into surgery.

Two casts were placed on me, four months prior to my wedding. And there I went, back into a storm. But I was alive and all I had to do was recover. I knew how to do that well. What I didn't know was this one would be a four-year journey with multiple surgeries and years in and out of a wheelchair, plus to this day, ambulating with a cane. I crushed two discs on my lower back. My foot would not bend, so I could not walk, and I developed chronic cellulitis—a bacterial infection that causes redness, swelling, and pain—from the crushing trauma to the left leg.

This time in my life, I truly had to take all my learnings and use them to carry on. I fought to stay in gratitude, open-mindedness, and perseverance. My internal awareness grew as I went through one setback after another. I understood that there were many paths to get to the end goal, and only through being open to change could I succeed. It carried into my work life. I became a change agent.

People would say, "How do you look at the situation so differently and come up with such good ideas?" I had no choice, but to try it a new way, because the standard path was not an option for me. The power of open-mindedness lets you listen to others in earnest and hone in on your creativity. It also lets you look at failure with a lens of empowerment. I still get chronic cellulitis episodes in my lower left leg. I know the routine and the antibiotics that I have to take, and I travel with a foldable cane at all times, just in case. It is part of my reality; it is part of my song of resiliency.

But this learning was truly about open-mindedness. We will get to resiliency later. It is the beautiful note in B flat. There were several songs, but I remember the first time I heard "Unpretty" by TLC. I could relate; it was a time of being judged by my mobility, and how I gained weight during this time. The stares and negative comments were all their problems, not mine, as I was beautiful inside and out, and I loved myself and was not spending the time living in someone else's lens. I was open to my future and the possibilities associated with each situation.

My son was now a married man and successful in his own small business. His wife, a wonderful woman that we are blessed to have as part of the family, brought an energetic, sweet, curly-haired bundle of joy to our lives. I knew that I was a mom, grandmother, wife, daughter, business woman, and volunteer for many causes, but I was still not sure what my true purpose was in this world. I was going to go through the darkest time in my life and I had no idea what was next.

It was a beautiful day on June the 14th. I was one month out to the day of my second hip replacement. The first one was five months prior and it was a great success. This time,

CHAPTER 1

the recovery was not as fast, but I was happy with the results. I put on a blue dress and sunglasses, and dropped the top down on my Mini Cooper, and off I went to get the hair done. As my hair stylist Gwen started applying my dye, I said, "I'm feeling unusual pain."

"Maybe some tea will help," she said, and she made me some.

I couldn't drink it. I tried going to the bathroom, but that was not working, either.

The pain felt like someone was stabbing me and strangling me at the same time in my gut. I got so hot, I had to peel my dress off; I could not stand having material on my body. Then, I fainted from the pain. Gwen called my husband, Bob, to come immediately. He did, and I awoke, screaming from the pain. She put a robe over me to get me to the car. The pain was worse and I was boiling from the fever.

"Let's go to the hospital," Bob said.

"No," I stupidly said. "All I want is to get in the shower."

Once home, he helped me into the shower, and down I went to the floor from the pain.

I screamed, "I'm dying, call an ambulance!"

When EMS arrived, a short woman entered my bathroom as I laid naked on the floor in pain, completely inconsolable. She looked at me, I screamed, "Help me!"

She looked at my husband and asked, "What drugs is she on?"

"No, my wife's not on medicine."

"No," the woman said. "I mean recreational drugs."

"No, we don't know what's going on. And no, she's not on anything."

It did not matter that I lived in a gated community with all the trappings of a successful professional. On that floor, they saw a Black woman who must have been a drug addict.

"Get up off the floor if you want to go to the ER," the woman ordered.

JOY NOTES

This angered my husband. "She can't without help!"

Two other EMS workers entered the bathroom and placed me on the stretcher. I was in deliria at that point and could not talk. All I did was groan in pain. I remember getting into the ambulance. That was my last memory until five days later.

EMS workers are incredible individuals and I would not be alive if it wasn't for their care, so I am not being negative or labeling. What amazed me was that I lived in one of the most expensive gated neighborhoods in Boston. Visitors had to pass through our gates to reach our home in this pristine golf community. And she had the audacity to see me as a drug addict because I'm a Black woman. The only reason I'm alive today is because my husband is Caucasian. When he told them to take me to the hospital, they did it because the request was coming from someone who looked like them. Otherwise, I would've still been that drug addict in their mind.

My husband, the surgeons, and the medevac team helped me piece together what happened next. I was taken to the closest hospital. This was a small community hospital in southern Massachusetts. They proceeded to do all the standard diagnostics, and finally did a CAT scan and identified that I had an abdominal obstruction. Time was of the essence, and they did not have the specialty to address my condition. My husband said I was awake during the identification process, and I requested to be transferred to Tufts Medical Center. The hospital contacted Tufts, where I was the Senior Vice President of Revenue Cycle, and requested a medevac transfer. While 10 minutes into the medevac ride, I had a cardiac arrest. The medevac team brought me back to life.

The trauma surgeons in the ER, Dr. Johnson and Dr. Bugaev, informed me that I was a mess when I came in. All tests and vitals were red. They took me into surgery and there was definitely sepsis. An hour into the surgery, I had

CHAPTER 1

my second cardiac arrest on the OR table. They placed me in extracorporeal membrane oxygenation (ECMO) to stabilize and strengthen me enough to make it through the surgery. I was in ECMO for 12 hours.

That morning was the Board meeting for Tufts Medical Center. Dr. Tarnoff, the CEO of Tufts Medical Center, received a text message that he was needed for a complex abdominal surgery during the board meeting. My boss at the time had no idea why I wasn't there, but that text let him know why. He excused himself from the meeting, as he had an emergency surgery to scrub into.

After being in ECMO, my labs and vitals all miraculously turned green; I could have surgery. They had to completely reconstruct me from the small intestine to the colon. I lost nine feet of intestine and looked like a jigsaw puzzle when they were done. I was placed in a chemically-induced coma for several days. They say every day in ICU equals a month of recovery time.

When I was brought back from the coma, I woke up in a room full of smiling faces. Dr. Tarnoff sat beside me and said, "You are one tough cookie."

"Ugh, what happened?" I had no idea, as my memory had stopped five days earlier after I had entered that ambulance in front of our house.

I awoke with a scar that extends from the top of my ribcage to my pelvis. There were fears that I would need a feeding tube and colostomy bag for the rest of my life. I had the feeding tube port from June through September. The colostomy bag was removed in August. Having had hip surgery a month prior to the catastrophe, I had to deal with major mobility problems. I lost the strength of my abdominal muscles. I had to build up muscle strength in my legs and abdominal cavity. I was older now; the body does not bounce back as fast as it once did.

Different than before, my friends were so supportive and my boss checked on me consistently. We had just kicked off our Epic implementation. My team had no experience in an enterprise build; I was so worried about them. Some called, telling me how scared they were of how things were going. I thought, *they need me. If I get busy and go back to work, I can get better sooner.* The first week of August, there was a big Epic onsite meeting and I decided that if my husband drove me and I had my cane, I could be there to support the team. Prior to the meeting, I had a feeding tube to hide and a colostomy bag to get rid of. I was lucky, progressing nicely and the home health nurse got the order to remove the bag before the meeting. This told me, "OK, you can get back to work." Of course, I did not ask my doctors if that was wise. I just did it.

I wore one of my favorite St. John's suits and Bob drove me to the Burlington Marriott where the event was held. Bob looked at me and asked, "Are you sure? You look tired from the ride."

"Absolutely," I said with true uncertainty. But if I didn't challenge myself, I would remain stuck in this bubble. I am my best cheerleader.

Every step was a momentary battle of will versus what my physical body could take. The walkways were longer than I remembered. I was finally in our room, committed to make it through the event. It was a struggle to concentrate, and my body was in pain. I remember hearing the Miss America song that Bob Barker would sing: "Smile though your heart is aching . . .". It kept me smiling. Somehow I made it through, but what mattered was that my team felt supported. I was able to give them the encouragement they were missing with the power of sincerity, authenticity, and validation of your teams' talents. They needed to be acknowledged for their feelings and opinions and validated that their talents were of substance and value. It was worth the trip.

CHAPTER 1

I came away from that meeting feeling the need to find my purpose. Why this chance at life after so much trauma? I decided to take a stab at driving again. I began by driving around my gated community to see how well I could handle my Mini Cooper. I put the top down and inhaled the cold air, my lungs filled with a sense of freedom. I felt hope and in need of exploration. My first venture outside of the development was a drive to Wollaston Beach, a mere three miles away from my home through beautiful, tree-lined streets that are quintessential New England loveliness. The trees were starting to peep in vibrant color early this year. So picturesque that it felt as if I were driving in a watercolor painting.

I got to the empty beach and parked. I put the top up and slowly took off my seatbelt as I stared forward, wondering, *What is next? I am so confused and lost.* I just sat there, took a deep breath, and opened the door. I scrambled to steady my cane on the ground and pulled myself slowly out of the car. I was wobbly, walking to the stone wall separating the sand from the sidewalk. It was 10 steps that tired me out and I gripped the wall for support. The view was cleansing and beautiful. The salt air heals and empowers.

As I leaned on the wall, I realized that I needed help. All my life through my traumas, I leaned into being resilient and powering forward. But what I did not do was deal with the trauma. I was not taught to acknowledge the trauma; I never saw my mother nor father accept that they were hurting or needed help.

The Queiro family never looked back as Celia Cruz would say, "No mires para atras para coger impulse" (Don't look back, not even to gain momentum). But that was wrong and it took me 50 years to understand it.

I needed to heal in order to help myself and others. My feet went into the cold sand and it made me shiver. But I embraced it as refreshing calmness. I closed my eyes and thanked God for this new chance at life.

I pulled my phone out of my hoody and texted Lora Carr, one of the most spiritually grounded individuals I've ever met. Lora answered the phone in her high-energy, beautiful voice: "Hi, how are you feeling?"

"Lora, I need help," I said. "I need to find a serenity place to heal."

"I got you!" Lora said. "Kripalu is where we need to go."

"I just want to be safe and be cared for in mind and body," I said.

She listened and let me be vulnerable without interruption. She knew that vulnerability was new to me and she was special in my heart for me to entrust my pain and fears with her.

When I stopped talking, she said, "We are booked. I've sent you the link so you can customize the experience. Because of the pandemic, Kripalu is only accepting 50% of the number of the occupants and things are a bit more intimate."

I was thrilled and scared all together. I had heard her stories of this respite that she went to with her sisters every year, but I never had done anything like it.

Two weeks later, I drove the two hours from my home to Kripalu Center for Yoga & Health in Stockbridge, Massachusetts. The moment I saw the sign that said, "Breathe, You've Arrived," and the beautiful grounds, I knew it was right. It was simple and peaceful.

I signed up for a workshop called, "Grief, Loss, Renewal." It was something that I normally would not have done, but I was here to walk into my life without limits. The room was large with cushions set up in a circle on the floor. Behind the circle were chairs with cushions. In a corner, there were cubbies full of blankets, cushions pencils and pads for notes. The sun flooded the room with natural light through many windows. It was a tranquil environment with lots of hurt people seeking help. You could feel tension and nervousness in the bodies as they took their places in the room.

CHAPTER 1

I wanted to hide in the back using my limited mobility as an excuse to sit outside of the circle, as I could not get on the floor. The session leader noticed that many tried to be outside of the circle and she surprised us by expanding the circle to include those in chairs, so we formed one larger circle.

This workshop was the first time that I openly stated my trauma and how lost I was. We had a partner exercise where we told our partner our story and they were not to speak, but instead to have direct eye contact and listen. First my partner spoke. I was not to react, but listen. It was so hard not to interrupt and try to fix her issues. She wasn't there to be fixed by me; she was there to free herself.

Then it was my turn to speak, and I noticed that I started whispering as I was scared to talk about how I was so uncomfortable with how people saw me as broken because my body had a malfunction. I talked about how people treated me as if I had no value or was not capable of the intelligence. No one saw my talents; they only saw the disability. People were rude and stopped making eye contact with me. Leaders would exclude me from conversations all of a sudden. This made me want to prove myself, but honestly it also made me tired of having to prove that my body got hurt, not my brain. I went deep on how I was seen in situations DIFFERENTLY.

I was able to look at others with an empathy that I never had before. I understood that many who were acting distant were merely in self-protection. Having to recognize me scared them, as I reminded them about how vulnerable we are and that we can't control all aspects of our life. Others saw my misfortune as an opportunity to expand their reach; they saw me as weak. I had people say to me that I no longer could handle the expectations of the job without ever talking to me, and making statements against my capabilities in my absence. It hurt deeply, but it also was the open door to my future. As I openly shared, I realized that I was OK to move forward. In those moments, I cried my loss and the feeling of insecurity and abandonment started to disappear.

After we finished telling our story, we provided a message to ourselves: if we were to go back in time prior to the trauma, what would we tell ourselves? I exhaled the gratitude of self-healing. This was just the beginning.

The Grief workshop gave me a surge of energy and I wanted more. Lora and I had made an agreement that we would create our own schedules and meet for silent breakfast and dinner. At dinner, however, I was invigorated. As we were talking about the options for the next day, there it was—meditative kayaking. I wanted to do it so bad, but I was not able to walk well and the idea of getting in and out of a kayak was terrifying. I told Lora that I wanted to do it, but knew it was not possible. She said rubbish. After dinner, we went to the front desk, and I slowly approached with my cane and horrible gait. The young lady at the desk said, "We are here to make your experience complete. Please come to the desk 20 minutes prior to the session."

"I can't walk to the beach or get into the kayak," I said.

"Breathe," she said. "We have you."

At noon, I arrived at the front desk and was greeted like a superstar. The head of the grounds came out and said, "Your chariot awaits, my lady."

I looked toward the door and there was a large golf cart. I walked to it and John helped me get in the cart. We rode through the perfectly manicured lawns through an opening in the woods. This path would have been impossible for me to maneuver on my own. Up and down through rocks, finally there was a clearing and I saw a beautiful beach and a kayak at the ready on the shore.

The golf cart stopped in front of the kayak; two gentlemen came over and helped me get out. They had my cane. I was 100% in their care. On the count of three, they lifted me and

CHAPTER 1

slid me into the kayak. I was reminded of how to place my feet and shift my weight, followed by a quick class about how to paddle. Minutes later, as the others got to the shore to get into their kayak, I was already in the water waiting for the group. The guides were giving directions. I could not hear the guide and asked for the group to move closer so I could hear. I now laugh that I screamed, "Hello, I can't hear!"

Everyone laughed and moved closer. Of course, the rest of the group had no idea why I was already in the kayak and that I was part of the group.

We started our journey. It was a slow start for me, as I was nervous that I could tip over. The water was like glass. It was a beautiful day with a bald eagle flying overhead as if he were protecting me from harm. We paddled in silence and the views were amazing. Big and small shore homes lined the lake, providing a history lesson of old and new, loved and neglected, similar to the stages that people are often in life. Lily pads and flowers floated on top of the glistening water. I found my peace.

There was this small island in the middle of the lake that had birds flying in and out and beautiful flowers surrounding it like a kaleidoscope of colors. I was drawn to it and— in a trance—paddled directly to it. Somehow I did not see the other kayak in front of me and I bumped into it. It was not a loud crash and it was not a serious enough bump, as we were moving slow. Unfortunately, the other kayaker thought it was a major tragedy.

"Are you stupid?" she screamed. "Hah! Yes, you! You don't belong here!"

"What? I'm sorry, I just didn't see you."

"Look where you are going, moron!"

My peace was gone. My greatest fear occurred: I was found out that I was not like everyone else, that I didn't belong—that I shouldn't be there—that disabled people don't get to kayak. Every negative thought came over me. The other kayaker was not the issue. I was the issue in that moment, and I opened the door to accept the words of her narrative. Frozen, I could not paddle. I did not know how to paddle anymore. My brain had lost all knowledge of basic moments. I was lost in anguish.

It seemed that out of nowhere, the other kayaker had appeared. Our guide came close and mentioned that it was her third week on the job. She said, "I often freeze in my head when things don't seem right. But from practice, I learned to just put the paddle in the water and make ripples happen. Ripples on the right and ripples on the left."

But I could not even place the paddle in the water. I was just frozen. The only thing that was moving were the tears rolling down my face. Her voice was faint in the cloud of my head. But she didn't give up on me. Next, my dear friend Lora came by with a rope and said, "Sometimes we need HELP."

"HELP me?" I asked. "No, I help others. I can't be towed in."

But she was right. I thought, *I'm a moron. I can't even paddle for myself.*

"We do this all the time for many reasons," Lora said. "We help each other. Why do you think the kayak has that loop? It's to click on and work together and tow each other."

She clipped on both kayaks, with the guide on my right and Lora as the fierce warrior towing ahead. We started moving.

"Want to make ripples?" the guide asked.

We laughed and for the first time, my paddle went into the water. The splash was quiet but powerful as it rang through my body. Without notice, I was paddling fast, first passing the guide, then passing Lora. Then I started towing her. We smiled as I passed her; she raised her paddle and made a gesture that she was now cruising and I was in charge. I towed her all the way to the shore. I owned my thoughts and my physical self while my spiritual connecting to nature blossomed. Throughout the kayaking trip, a beautiful eagle had been flying above us, coming low and close, then soaring high. As we came in, the eagle circled above us and I interpreted this majestic bird as the Lord, my protector, watching over me.

When we arrived on shore, my three helpers were waiting for me. I greeted them with a big smile and said, "I am ready for my magical carpet ride." They laughed and helped me out of the kayak. They gave me my cane and I slowly walked to the SUV that they drove down to the beach. They had decided it would be a better ride than the cart.

As I reached the SUV, the lady who had screamed at me opened the door to get into the vehicle.

"I'm sorry," said a voice behind me. "This is a reserved transport."

"I'm tired and need a ride to the main building," said the lady who had called me stupid and a moron.

"Sorry, this is a reserved vehicle," repeated the voice behind me.

The lady slammed the door and gave me a dirty look. I moved forward and got inside the vehicle. I was fine, I embraced help, I owned my mind body and spirit, and I was ready to move forward. I realized that I needed to not be distracted with other people's fears and insecurities projected on me. I told myself, *I have to believe in myself and hold on to my peace and grace.* This learning took me forward as the recovery continued.

When I returned to work, I was dedicated to lead with the empathy that was not given to me. I wanted to set the example of the empathetic leader that provided the safe space for my team members to thrive. That meant seeing every individual as their whole self and understanding the generational differences and needs.

We had individual and team leadership training and really focused on understanding each others' talents. That meant that some of the position responsibilities changed and we celebrated the triumphs and valued the failures as great opportunities of growth. The team was humming and the financials yielded the highest financial cash collections in history. Inside the world of Revenue Cycle life was thriving.

Unfortunately, my new approach was foreign to the organizational culture outside of my departments. Even though we yielded the highest engagement scores in the organization, the feedback from the executive leadership was negative. I had created a team that had outpaced the organization. While my people were doing very well, the rest were not in alignment. I learned that it is important to understand the course of change that the organization is able to handle. You must support the overall organizational pace. And you must respect their pace while staying authentic to your leadership style. I'm forever grateful to my boss at the time for supporting my decision to focus on my purpose.

We were too different and I knew I had to follow the path that was my purpose. I started my journey to leave the comfortable and step into my purpose. This was a difficult decision, but it was the right decision.

After that time in Kripalu, I did a great deal of praying to understand why I was here for another chance. Give back, be the support the light that you did not have. Use your talents to make a difference in underserved communities and help others that look like you advance in their careers. So, I set out to become an executive coach and get as much AI training as possible. I needed to be worthy of stepping in the gap with sound knowledge and advice.

I contacted the sagest person that I know, Dr. Malynn Utzinger. Malynn is a beam of light; she can provide guidance and understanding through the toughest times. She was my therapist in my time of need and she is a friend. She listened and smiled.

"I knew you would come to this point eventually," she said.

"What?"

"It was part of your purpose," she said, "you just needed the time to be ready."

I cried as I went on a mental journey of the multiple times that I thought I had needed to make a change to purpose, and here it was. There was no turning back. Malynn introduced me to IPEC, as she believed that this was the best program for me based on who I was.

I went on my journey to self-awareness, education, and preparedness for the future. I started setting up my business, and January 30th was my last day in corporate healthcare.

NIO'S FOUR TIPS FOR SURVIVING & THRIVING WITH JOY

I shared my story, along with tips on how to overcome and live joyously, no matter what's happening in your life. Everyone has their own formula, and here is mine:

1. Meditate and Pray. Stay connected to spirit.

2. Find your joy in music. Listening, playing, dancing, watching people enjoy it.

3. I have to believe in myself and hold on to my peace and grace.

4. Follow your passion. I left my corporate career in healthcare to become a healthcare consultant and motivational speaker. This took tremendous courage and confidence, because being an entrepreneur is a high risk endeavor. A speaking career can succeed or fail. It requires stepping way out of a comfort zone with a steady paycheck and benefits for health care and retirement. You are on your own and your success depends upon YOU.

And as someone who has had many health crises, I have to be physically able to travel frequently and stand on stages where I give it my all—mentally, physically, and spiritually. My lifestyle of traveling, speaking, and conducting training requires a huge energy expenditure. But I am fully committed to it, because this is my passion. So, even on days when I am beyond exhausted, I find the energy within myself to compose and deliver the most powerful messages possible, because this work is my God calling.

It comes from my heat and my soul. It is my mission to share with the world, to uplift and inspire people everywhere, drawing upon the trauma of my own experiences, and the lessons learned along the way, to help everyone I meet, learn how to triumph over their own challenges, physical or otherwise.

CHAPTER 2

Salsa: Finding Your Rhythm— My Father's Story

Salsa: a Latin American musical genre that means "hot sauce" and fuses Cuban dance music with elements of American and Puerto Rican qualities with a fast tempo, simple repetitive beats, and a festive spirit.

Salsa is the music that truly brought my dad's magnetic personality to life. When we went to weddings, the ladies would line up to dance with "El Salsero Tony," a master of the art of dancing salsa. Why salsa? Because the music is a source of fearless emotion. This music is rooted in Afro-Cuban rhythm and song, "Son Cubano." My father was the essence of Salsa.

When I was four years old, my family migrated to the United States. It was a journey that provided us freedom from oppression, opportunity, access to healthcare, and a new life we could have never imagined.

My family needed this health care after my father had an accident in the sugar cane fields in Cuba. He lost his sight in one eye and became fragile from multiple infections. My mom, the queen of resiliency and imagination, was not accepting the situation. She did her research. Dear reader, can you pause for a minute and think about how difficult it was to do research during the late sixties and seventies before the Internet?

Being the resourceful woman that she was, my mom was able to find a program through the American Red Cross that could potentially get my dad an eye transplant. But to come to America, we would need a sponsor. The sponsor had to be a relative who would provide lodging and financial security for 10 years for a family of five: Mom, Dad, my two brothers, and me (the youngest and only girl).

We did not know of any family in the United States, but my mom had friends who had access to phone books and a Cuban network. After months of letter-writing, a stranger with our blood line took a chance on our little family—sight unseen—against his wife's advice. Mario was a tall, white, blue-eyed Spaniard living in New Jersey.

It was February 10th when we heard the knock on the door and we were informed that it was our time to go to the airplane hangar and wait for our seats on the plane to the USA. We were there for a day and a half. Even as a four-year-old, I remember the waiting and how I was trying so hard to keep my white linen dress clean so I would look pretty when we got to this unknown place called America.

We got on the plane, which took us to Miami, Florida. We were shuttled to another hanger, where we were processed and checked for diseases. We got our shots and then waited. It was as if we were an Amazon package (decades before the Amazon system was ever created), waiting for someone to claim us.

Finally, after a few days, we were told we were going to NYC. It was February and we had no idea what was ahead. I remember getting on the train and being amazed by all the experiences in a short week: leaving the family in Cuba, flying to a strange country, and now riding a train. As a child, this was a wonderland moment.

CHAPTER 2

We arrived at Grand Central Station in New York City. What a huge place! The air was so very cold; it was a new sensation that scared me. The reason we were there was that my dad was so frail. My mom was so poised as she navigated caring for three kids and a sick husband who had only 20% of his vision. Always calm and collected, he never complained.

Mom had a picture of Mario, so we recognized him as we ascended from the gate. He was holding a sign with our name, so we walked towards him—a light-skinned Afro-Cuban who had a dark-skinned Afro-Cuban wife and kids.

"This family does not look like me," he said, "but you're part of me."

Mario hugged us as if we were his close, LONG LOST FAMILY MEMBERS. It was a safe place; we were acknowledged as worthy.

We went outside and the cold—which I had never felt in tropical Cuba—was unbelievable. We went to a local church in Spanish Harlem and were given coats and winter clothes. Then we were off to the New York Eye and Ear Infirmary of Mount Sinai, where my dad was admitted. Then we went to a building on 110th Street between Amsterdam and Broadway, where my mom was to be the superintendent of the building. We lived in the basement apartment. It was a scary place, but my mom gave me and my brothers our rules of engagement: we were to always be together, and none of us could be left behind.

My mom took us to the library, and we checked out phonic books. We watched *Sesame Street,* having been told we needed to know enough English to meet acceptance into the local grammar school. A few weeks later, Mom took us to school, and we all tested above grade average and were placed in classes above our age level and no ESL (English as a Second Language). I went to first grade at age four-and-a-half. Henry was three years older and went to third grade and Rafael, at age nine, attended fifth grade. Having a math educator as a mom meant that we all knew our times tables and long division at age four.

As we acclimated to life in the States, my dad was not successful with the eye transplant. He faced a decision about whether he should be on total disability, which meant he could not work. Receiving a government disability check each month would not provide enough income to provide for a wife and three children.

So, my father chose to care for his family against all odds. He would bandage his eye daily and go to work at a factory to make the money required to care for us. After being robbed multiple times in the basement apartment, he was referred to a job in New Jersey, where he worked at United Hospital in Union City, New Jersey. United became Palisades General Hospital and he worked there for 30 years. He went to work in a suit every day. And he finally got a glass eye and he was a source of positive influence to all he touched.

When salsa music played, he would have to take a few salsa steps to acknowledge the sound of an energizing breath of release. Nothing is not possible in the sounds of salsa.

When my dad passed, he was in a skilled care facility. Smiling and talking to his roommate as he laughed with vigor, he took his last breath. It was such a perfect way for him to go to the other side in Joy. For his funeral, so many people contacted us, volunteering to assist us. It was overwhelming. It is Cuban tradition to provide refreshments at the wake. We were blessed with donations from restaurant owners because it was Tony who passed. His signing book and digital site have hundreds of notes and stories about the impact that he had made on other's lives. The funeral home was filled to capacity with politicians, C-suite leaders, business owners, and people of all means speaking many languages. He was a change agent and I'm proud to be his daughter.

CHAPTER 2

During his wake, we played his beloved salsa. Some danced in his honor. Others told stories. It was an awakening for us about how you can make a difference, one person at a time. As I worked on the thank you cards, I noted a theme. Three key leadership principles that he embodied resonated in the notes and stories I read.

MY FATHER'S THREE TIPS FOR SURVIVING & THRIVING JOY

My father's story illustrates how *Joy Notes* filled him with happiness that he shared with everyone around him. Here are his three tips for surviving and thriving through life's challenges.

- Trust
- Lead
- Respect

Trust. My father created a culture of **trust** with everyone who was in his presence. He was intentional about everything he said and did. He defined trust as caring for the relationship and emotions of others by being present and kind in your actions and words. He was consistently aware of his behavior and even when things were chaotic, he lived his beliefs of kindness and safety for everyone within the situation.

Leadership. My dad's second theme was about Honoring Leadership. He believed that at all times, you should recognize and acknowledge the worth of others and bring out the best in them, listening purposefully to engage in the solution while demonstrating kindness.

Respect. The last theme was Respect, the key to his nature and ability to having the courage to influence. This means never leading with fear or worry, or falling into self-preservation tactics that Discount others as not as important as your need for superiority. Dad respected people and led with a smile. He welcomed others, acknowledging and validating them where they stood. He did not judge. He was curious and always sought to understand how he could help.

Salsa was his *Joy* and a tool to invite others to celebrate joy with him.

My father also had the courage to make difficult choices, such as deciding not to accept disability and instead working full-time to provide for his family.

In addition, my dad seized every opportunity to indulge his passion for his beloved Salsa music, breaking into a happy, radiant state and dancing, which inspired everyone around him to share his joyous moment.

CHAPTER 3

The Blues—Out of Pain Comes Power

The Blues: Melancholic music that orginated in African American folk culture, characterized by a 12-bar sequence. It was born in the rural South of the United States near the close of the 19th century. Its popularity expanded during the 1940s during the Great Migration as Black people moved to cities. This birthed the urban blues, which evolved into Rhythm and Blues and Rock 'n Roll.

The Blues are about speaking from the soul and moving into perseverance against all odds. That describes my friend, **Darcel McCullough**. She's had so many mishaps in her life. Yet there she is, just like The Blues, overcoming obstacles that seem impossible. That's the theme of Blues songs, which wrap words and musical notes around every human being's power to succeed against the odds, including in love and romance. One of my favorite Blues songs is "Woman You Must Be Crazy" by T Bone Walker.

The Blues express confidence where there should be no confidence.

This genre originated during an era in American history when society was toying with the idea of changing laws to end the horrific institution of slavery. During that time, some Black people got a glimpse of freedom. Limited freedom, but freedom to some degree. Still, most remained brutally oppressed.

The Blues expressed the horrors of this reality. It was the music in the gap. It was the music of perseverance.

Today, my dear friend Darcel is sharing her story to illustrate the power of this perseverance.

She's a Special Education Resource Teacher for the North Bergen School District in New Jersey. This amazing lady is also pursuing her PhD in Special Education.

Darcel and I met when she was Pre-Med at Temple University. At the time, we belonged to the same church group. Darcel is a gifted singer, and her voice fills a room with joy. Her smile is infectious and she loves her friends and family in such a special way that you feel honored to be part of her tribe.

When I asked her to share her story of overcoming trauma with a song in her heart, she was shy yet called to provide insights that can help you find your Joy Notes in the midst of trauma so that you, too, can triumph over life's most difficult hurdles.

Niobis Queiro: Ms. Darcel, thank you so much for your time and joining me. I know that you have a very special story about illness and how you were able to come through and not let it bind you.

Right now, you're going through a PhD program, and you put that illness in the background. But in life, you've gone through so much and it's never stopped you. I would love to hear one of those lovely stories from you. Please tell me about your trauma, how you were close to death, and how you were able to bring yourself through.

Darcel: A little background. Being a lupus patient, my immune system was already compromised. In October of 2021, I

CHAPTER 3

contracted RSV, which is a respiratory virus. In November, I had multiple blood clots in both lungs and one in my left calf muscle, and was put on Eliquis, the blood thinner. On December 19th, I was diagnosed with COVID. I didn't have any symptoms, so I thought, *Well, this is great. I'm asymptomatic.* About five days later, it hit me like a ton of bricks. I felt the upper respiratory symptoms of a cold. I had trouble breathing. I was coughing, had mucus, sinus issues. But I felt very lethargic, very tired.

I noticed that I was having problems catching air, unable to catch my breath, unable to get air. Because I had COVID, I was staying away from my family. So, I missed Christmas. I missed New Year's.

They were calling me, but I was sleeping so much that, oftentimes, I wouldn't answer the phone. They knew there was a problem, because I never missed calling my family on New Year's Eve. And so, my oldest son did a wellness check and the police came and they woke me up.

I said, "Oh, I'm fine."

That's what I kept saying: "I'll be fine." Because I've always gotten over things. I've been down and out with the lupus. I've had a heart attack. I've had lung issues.

Just different organs have been affected because of lupus, and I've always gotten over it. I was fine. But I should have known there was a problem when I would get up from the sofa to go to the bathroom. I would make it to the bathroom and then realize that, *Oh, wow.* Now I would try to catch my breath. Then, after going to the bathroom, I'd make it back to the sofa and I was fighting. I was literally punching and kicking the air to try to breathe.

I knew, *Something is really wrong here.* Then, I lost control of my bowels twice going to the bathroom. I found myself laying on the floor, cleaning the floor with Clorox and towels, and then laying there sleeping. I wasn't laying in the mess, but I was just sleeping there for a while, then getting back to the sofa.

On January 2nd, my friends were calling me from time to time. I would say, "Well, you know, I'm having a little bit of trouble breathing." To me, it was just a little trouble breathing.

There's this little thing called air, and I told my son that I was having a hard time getting it.

"I'm coming to get you," he said, and took me to the hospital. Had he not taken me then, they probably would have found me in a day or two in that apartment. They would have found my body, we'll just put it like that.

When I got to the hospital, they got me into a room in the emergency room. But they said they no longer had the antibody serum [that] they were giving people . . . for five days along with steroids. They [gave me oxygen].

It wasn't enough oxygen. They put the mask on. That didn't seem to be giving enough. They were about to intubate. I said, *God, they cannot intubate me. Too many people are dying. They aren't coming off [ventilators]. I have to breathe.*

I started trying my best just to get air. I kept coughing and coughing and I just couldn't catch it.

All of a sudden, the nurse came in—smiling because they received a shipment of the antibody treatment, and she goes:

"You're not getting intubated. You're going on the treatment."

She hooked me up to the IV and they did that. But during that time, I was still having trouble breathing. I was just laying there and I kept telling myself:

You cannot be a statistic. This is not how you die. You are not a COVID victim. Your children are not burying you and saying, "My mother died of COVID." This is not how you die. This is not the end of your story.

I prayed, but I remember having a very, very deep, deep talk with the Lord. It was spirit and spirit [mine and His].

My body wasn't there [when I heard the Lord ask,] "Are

you ready? Even if it is your time, are you even ready?"

[I responded,] I believe, yes, but am I done here? Am I done with what you want me to do?

I remember very clearly the Lord saying, "Are you ready to come?"

I said, "I want to make sure my one son is really walking in his purpose."

The Lord said, "Then you're not ready."

I said, "Oh, wait a minute, Lord." Then I thought I said, "But I have to give him over to you. He's yours and I have to wait. I have to truly give him to you. I've prayed, I've done what I could. I've raised him up in the way that he should go. But I have to give him to you, so if this is . . . I don't believe it's my time to go. But yeah, I'm ready to walk into eternity with you, Lord, and let you take care of my family."

That was the one thing that I needed . . . to know that I was ready to really walk away from this life by being able to let go of my family, to say, "God, if you can't let go of them here, you're not ready to go. Is it for me?"

Nio: What turned it around so that you could . . . experience that "aha" moment, that peace in that moment. But what made you say, "I've let this go, it's in your hands. But I got more to do." What made you push to stay?

Darcel: When I got peace in knowing that [my son] Juan was His. [God's]. [I said,] "I gave him to you, he is yours." I had peace with that. I had fear that Juan wasn't His.

Nio: I got you.

Darcel: I was walking in that promise that me and my household will serve their promises that we thought that He has given to us to those who love, who are called. I have to stand on that. There are things that have been told to me, that He has told me, that He has sent prophets to tell me. There are things that have been said that I have to stand on.

Am I going to stand? Is it that I am going to be unstable in all my ways? Am I going to vacillate between one decision or another? Or am I going to believe what His words tell me . . . no matter what the circumstances look like? Is it going to be faith? Am I going to see it? Am I going to believe it before I see it? Do I have to see it to believe it?

I was able to say, "He is yours." I let that go.

Now what more do I need to accomplish here in this life? So I can go [die], but this is not how it's going to happen. Not this. Oh no. Not this evil thing that the devil has cooked up. This is not it.

I felt myself fighting to come back. In that apartment, I was dying. I saw it after I got to the hospital. Because what I was feeling was actually my life going from me and I didn't know it. I needed to be taken to the hospital.

Once I got to the hospital, my mindset thought that I might still be dying because they were going to put me on a ventilator and I knew that people were not coming off those machines and dying. Once I got to the hospital, it was okay. *You're going to live now.* I had to come to that place where I'm going to fight to live. It was already set up, but my mind hadn't gotten there yet.

Nio: You had to catch up.

Darcel: I had to catch up. It was a battle, still. I could not talk without coughing. Every time I opened my mouth to say a word, I just coughed. It was painful. I couldn't do anything. I couldn't shower. I couldn't wash. I'm a person who has dry skin and I have to lotion. Didn't care. I had alligator feet and alligator skin.

I had . . . crust on my feet when I finally got to shower and all. It was horrible. But you just don't care. You're alive. That's right and that's all that matters. So, I spent eight days in the hospital on oxygen. I'm still on oxygen. I get taken to a nursing home . . . put in the COVID ward. I have to stay there until I get a negative COVID diagnosis. I'm there for occupational therapy and physical therapy.

I'm there for about a month. They're working on my oxygen. OT is basically your occupation in life . . . to take care of yourself. That's what they're helping me to do, and physical therapy to build up. That was going very well. When I left, I left there without oxygen. Yeah, I really worked and did whatever I needed to do.

They taught me how to do bird baths from the sink with a chair. I learned how to do that bird bath with my wheelchair, to get clean without passing out, because I would take the oxygen out and forget to put it back in when I stood up and stuff like that. When I first got to the hospital and I would stand, they would put the commode right next to me. As soon as I stood up, my oxygen just plummeted.

The nurses came running. "What happened? What are you doing?"

I said, "I just wanted to sit on the commode and go to the bathroom."

They are like, "No. You can't do that. You have to call us and we will come and put you on the commode."

That happened a couple of times, and I was like, "I'm sorry, I forgot, I just wanted to go." But my oxygen just kept dropping every time I would get up. They want you to have at least 95, and it was below 80.

That wasn't good. But when I was in the nursing home, it started to stay around 88. They said, "Okay, "If you can get it above 90, then maybe we can really work with you, with maybe not having to go home with oxygen, or at least go home with it intermittently."

Anyway, I got it to the point where I didn't have to go home with oxygen. However, the brain fog was really an issue, and my pulmonologist said, "I wonder if perhaps you're losing oxygen at night. If you're still suffering so badly from brain fog, you could be losing oxygen at night."

We did a sleep apnea test. I do not have sleep apnea. I've been tested three times for sleep apnea.

"I'm telling you," I told my doctor, "I don't have it."

He was so funny. When the results came in, he said, "I'm going to tell you something. I owe you an apology. I didn't say this to your face, but I was thinking, *'She's got sleep apnea.'* You do not have sleep apnea. You are so far from sleep apnea. But you are losing oxygen at night. You are in between 83 and 87%, and that is not good."

I am still on oxygen at night. Sometimes a lot of times, I forget to put it on. I realized that I still need it, because sometimes I'll wake up during the night, and I'm like, *Oh, that's not a good feeling.*

I'm on oxygen at night and I am using crutches right now. One of my discs, which I've never had this issue, I have a herniated disc that is crushing my sciatic nerve, which has pain generating down into my right leg.

They didn't know what the problem was, and I couldn't get an MRI, because insurance made me jump through hoops, telling me, "You've got to go through therapy. You've got to see this doctor, that doctor."

I was going through physical therapy, but every time I would do physical therapy, I would wind up in more pain. Then, two or three days after therapy, right before I would go back, I couldn't walk. I was in so much pain. I'm like, "What's going on?"

Finally, [they told me], "You have this disc that's pressing on this nerve. You really should be seeing a chiropractor.

They wanted me to go for pain management, but I thought, *If I go for pain management, and they give me medication, they're going to mask the pain and I'm not going to get cured, and I could be messing it up even more. So I'm going to the chiropractor.*

I am still experiencing pain, but it's lessening. I was using a walker, then I went to a cane, but then it got worse, because I was climbing a lot of stairs for work. Now I'm using crutches, because I'm able to put more weight onto the crutches instead of the leg.

Nio: Better weight distribution.

Darcel: Though, I will lay the crutches down and walk around a little bit, just to get my legs used to being not so dependent upon the crutches. But I enjoy what I do. I'm a teacher, a special ed teacher.

I love what I do. I don't feel like I work. That pushes me to get up every day, even with the pain, because it's worse in the morning. It hurts to get up and hurts to sit down. Mind you, I get up, and you have to get up and sit down all throughout the day. You have to go to the bathroom. It hurts to go to the bathroom, hurts to sit down in a chair, stand up, get in the car, get out.

Sometimes, I just want to sit there and say, "I don't want to go to the bathroom." Sometimes, I wait, and that's why I wear Depends [adult diapers], because it takes me a while to get to the bathroom, so I make sure what I wear Depends just in case I don't make it, and there are many times that I don't. That's another issue that I deal with, and I had to get past the pride thing, was the Depends.

Nio: I mean, if you were to share with other women, how do you keep going on? What is that lesson learned in life? As something so debilitating, it's in your midst. You mentioned the most important phrase in the world that we all have to learn is **letting go of pride.** What else?

Darcel: You have to find that thing within you that makes you who you are. This is me and this is what makes me who I am, that makes life for me.

I know, first of all, **I'm a child of the King, so I'm not a failure, ever.** No matter what comes my way, I'm not a failure, because I'm his. Whatever comes my way, if that doesn't work for me, it wasn't for me. Over here, maybe it was for me. So that wasn't what I failed, it's just something else for me, and so what makes me live? What's life for me? That's what keeps me going.

I found teaching. I love children. I mean, **I'm crazy about my children and they're 38 and 35.** But when you hear me talk about them, you think they'd be three or four. They're just my babies, always going to be. And now I have grandchildren. I'm just over the moon.

Nio: Thank you for teaching my grandchild.

Darcel: Yes. I'm so excited that I had your grandson in my Sunday school class. I'm just looking at him like he's going to say, "Something's wrong with her. Grandma's lady kept staring at me today in church, because she was seeing me."

When they say, **love what you do**, you'll never work a day in your life. That's me. I love going to work. It's not work for me. It's not a job for me. I love the children that I interact with. I love teaching them. I love seeing them grow. I love talking with them. Even the "smart aleck" teenagers that I've had to deal with. I fall in love with them. That's who I am. That's my purpose. When you also discover your purpose, there are many things that I am here to do. Teaching is one of them. Worship leader.

Nio: I was just going to go there, because you have a long history in music. I mean, backup singer for Gloria Gaynor. A worship leader like no other. But always blessed by your voice. Through this, what music was in your head? You know how we have that song? While going through the muck, it keeps us going. What was that for you?

Darcel: Oh, my goodness. Let me tell you. **In every season of my life, there have been songs that have pulled me through.** There are certain songs that I will hear and I will play. I mean, over and over and over again. There was a song, which is really something that after the fact, [and the lyrics are about God putting His breath in my lungs so I can praise Him].

That has meant so much to me, because my lungs were deficient. They were deficient of air. It's His air that we breathe. If it wasn't for Him, we wouldn't be here. He breathed life into us.

Darcel: Oh, my goodness. After I learned that, **it's [God's] breath in our lungs**, I came through that. His breath meant so much more to me. Worship means so much more to me, because when you've been close to death and now you're here and you're able to worship, you're able to, again, tell someone, "You can make it!"

I did. It just makes life so much sweeter. You appreciate your walk, you appreciate what you went through, and you appreciate God so much more. I find that I am on the flip side of joy so much more. You have your days. I don't have those days like that. Hardly ever.

I was in a great deal of pain from head to toe. When I first came home from the hospital from the nursing home, there were many days when I was alone by myself in that apartment. That was very lonely. I shed tears because of physical pain, but had joy and peace that I cannot explain to you. That piece surpasses all understanding. I was like, "Oh, I'm going to die." Even now with the pain, like sometimes I go to get out of the car . . . it hurts.

But I say, "Hey, I'm alive. I'm here. Thank you, Jesus!"

I'm going to live and I'm going to live joyfully. **I choose joy.** I really do. Especially after all that.

Nio: Thank you. Thank you for choosing joy, giving joy, and walking in His steps. There is still so much for you to do.

Darcel: Amen!

DARCEL'S THREE TIPS FOR SURVIVING & THRIVING WITH JOY

Darcel personifies the power of The Blues, the music of confidence and perseverance when for some, all hope may be lost. The soulful sounds of The Blues are deeply spiritual, and it was Darcel's faith that brought her back from the brink of death, and empowered her to recover and resume the life that she loves as a teacher.

All the while, her favorite songs provided resilience in her spirit, as well as her mind and body, to heal and thrive. Her goal is to help you move forward when all seems impossible.

Here are her three tips for finding your *Joy Notes* when you need them most:

- **Let go of pride.**

- **Find your passion/purpose.**

- **Have deep faith.**

Let go of pride and ego. They serve no one for good. Pride will stop you from asking for and receiving the resources you need. In her story, Darcel shared the deeply personal reality that she relies on adult diapers because, due to her pain and slower mobility, she cannot always make it to the bathroom in time.

Find your passion and purpose. Your passion releases an energy in your system that makes you feel authentic. It creates moments when you can't stop smiling, your heart beats a little faster, and you know that your passion and purpose are your reason for being. This is yours and no one can tell you what it is.

For Darcel's educational journey, she first went to university for dance, then liberal arts, but even after receiving her degree, she was not fulfilled until she found Special Ed. So, she earned her Master's Degree that was aligned with her passion, and now she's completing her PhD in Special Ed. When she speaks about her kids in her classes, she is on fire with passion and purpose as an advocate, educator, caregiver, friend, advisor, and all-encompassing practitioner.

She gives her heart and soul to her students, because teaching is her passion and purpose. This enables you to stop focusing on the past pain and instead focus on the meaning happening in the present moment.

Have deep faith. Darcel's health challenges illustrate her faith in God to pull her through even life-threatening circumstances.

She has also applied her deep faith to challenges during her ambitious quest for higher education.

One day, we were talking about what was new in our lives, and she told me about her class issues. She did not understand how to meet the requirement that her professor was requesting to succeed in a statistics course. It was a communication issue and understanding the course material.

As she told me the story, I said, "You know that I used to teach statistics as part of the financials course in the MPH program that I was an adjunct for at two universities."

The next thing that naturally came out of my mouth was, "How can I help?"

"I need help," she said, showing that Pride was not a player here.

"Would you like some tutoring sessions?" I asked.

"Yes, please, but you're busy, so how?"

"We will figure it out," I said.

The next week, we scheduled our first session on Sunday after church. We meet every week around both our busy schedules, I helped her find her way through the world of statistics and she was able to exceed her professor's expectations.

In the course, students were graded on a system of 880 points. She needed 612 points to get a C. And at week 9, she was at 407 points. The week 9 assignment was worth 60 points, and week 10 and 11 combined had 160 points. The remaining work was worth 220 points. She needed to yield 205 points to earn a C. The final was 212 points.

"I got a Flat C that felt like an A," Darcel informed me in a text message.

Standing in faith, the calvary came to Darcel's rescue to her achieve the goal she set. She learned statistics, passed her class, and did not ruin her GPA.

Yes, we had a strategy and a plan, but faith and hope kept us persevering in the face of adversity.

CHAPTER 4

Hip Hop—Misunderstood

Hip Hop: a musical genre and culture born in the 1980s and 1990s as an anti-drug and anti-violence artform that evolved into dance, graffiti, and a global movement of self-expression, unity, and self-determination. Created by African American youth on the playgrounds of the Bronx in New York City, Hip Hop fuses drumming, powerful messaging, and a poetic rhythm of speaking that became wildly popular and diverse.

Whether you remember the lyrics about Hip Hop from Keef Cowboy or The Sugar Hill Gang in "Rapper's Delight," it was the start of something powerful and beautiful. This genre of music originated in 1970s by Black American and Caribbean American youth in the Bronx in New York as a vocal expression of an anti-drugs and anti-violence genre. The rhythmic drumbeats delivered poetic speech and told the stories of the voiceless, blasting in basement house parties, block parties, and schoolyard competitions.

This music was a culture. It was innovative, as it mastered the use of primitive technology with scratching, remixing songs, sampling, and using drum machines. Nothing was off limits to create unique beats that gave us break dancing, rapping, fashion, and a global phenomenon in every language imaginable.

I remember being a kid in West New York, New Jersey, listening to WBLS and hearing the Sugar Hill Gang for the first time and pulling out a pen and paper to write down the lyrics. Then I would wait by the radio—in a trance—until they played it again. It was the buzz in school, dance class, and anywhere kids gathered.

Unfortunately, Hip Hop has been profoundly misunderstood. People have tainted it with a negative connotation. Hip Hop originated as a modern spin on storytelling and communication on urban playgrounds. All these kids in projects weren't interested in doing anything bad. They just wanted to have a voice, a means of communicating with each other. It did not come from thug life.

However, about a decade into the Hip Hop era, some of the guys who were performing Hip Hop on the playgrounds went to jail and created a new culture of Hip Hop inspired by their experiences while locked up.

This vilified the genre with a reputation that it glorifies violence, thugs, misogyny, crime, and prison life.

This was not the plan for Hip Hop; its origin is innocent and happy.

The year that I discovered Hip Hop, I was going to Cuba with my mom for the first time since we had left the country in 1970. Laws had changed, allowing us to go visit. My mom wanted to take me to celebrate my Quinces—my 15th birthday—in Cuba amongst the family. In our culture, the Quinces party—or Quinceañera—celebrates a girl's passage into womanhood.

I remember that trip as if it were yesterday. I felt the anxiety of going to a land that was somewhat fictional to me because I had left it as toddler. All I had was second-hand knowledge of the country through stories told by my parents. I was going to meet strangers whom I was to embrace

CHAPTER 4

as family and then I was to have a party to celebrate coming of age in a foreign world, apart from my friends and all that I knew to be normal for an American teenager. Fantastic!!

I remember all the bags that we packed. We had two bags each, but they were extra-large military duffle bags. The bags were considered "gusanos"—which means worms—because the bags were large and conformed to the shape of whatever was packed inside.

We came to our homeland bearing gifts. Back then, these trips were about bringing as many clothes, dry goods, and medicine as possible within the luggage weight restrictions. The Cuban government financially exploited the returning "traitors" or Cuban exiles. We had to pay several thousands of dollars for the travel visa, then we paid a tax on the goods that we brought with us, based on the preserved value of the items.

As a kid, I stood beside my mom in a room filled with tables and families surrounding their bags as the Customs Officers went through every item in our bags. It was unreal to watch them pulling the items that they wanted for themselves—and we could not say anything. It was hot. The air was heavy with the smell of human sweat and dread. My mom was calm through it all. She smiled and we got most of our items through. Mom was wise to the Customs game, thanks to speaking to her friends who had done the voyage before.

Because of that, we were dressed in layers (before it was a thing). We had on three shirts, two pairs of pants, and a jacket in 89-degree weather. This was the only way for two females to transport male clothes at the time. As a result, we were boiling from the heat. Can you say, "Hot, hot, hot?"

One of the funniest moments was when a Ziploc bag of Tang powdered drink mix busted open and they initially thought it was drugs. Guards swarmed our table.

"Please taste it," my mom calmly said.

They did and asked, "What is it?"

"It's powdered medicine for my daughter to drink in the morning," she said.

They all looked at me and I smiled, casting a puppy dog stare for extra effect. P.S.: I hate Tang.

Finally, we made it to the hotel, where we received our indoctrination into the rules and regulations surrounding our visit. We were at the Hotel Nacional, one of the premier hotels in Old Havana. It was like stepping back into an old Hollywood movie from the 50s. They had cigarette girls in the lobby, bellmen dressed in uniforms with the beanie hats, and doormen wearing white gloves and topcoats.

I was amazed to witness the two Cubas: the dismal Cuba where people were struggling to get a morsel of food, and the luxurious Cuba that was provided to the tourist. I didn't belong at either end of the spectrum. I was Cuban-born, but an American, and I wasn't your average tourist. I was there to reunite with *mi familia.*

In the group that we were placed in, there was another girl my age and the rest were adults. Maria was from Miami. She, too, was going to celebrate her Quinces with her estranged *familia.* We saw each other across the room, and like synchronized swimmers, we both asked our moms if we could sit together. It was a moment of glee. We got a table for two, introduced ourselves, and talked over each other, as we were so full of emotion:

Do you believe that customs nonsense?
Crazy, right?!
Are you wearing multiple outfits?
Yes, dying to take a shower.
Where are you from?
Miami, New Jersey.
Are you going to be staying at the hotel or with family?

CHAPTER 4

With family, it's all about the Quinces experience in Cuba.
Are your scared?
Terrified.
What's your favorite song?

This question sparked our moment of escape and pure joy. We held hands, our smiles lit-up the room, and in perfect beat, we sang at the top of our lungs the lyrics of "Rapper's Delight." That became our anthem for the trip. All the voices in the room stopped as we sang the whole song with the lyrics intact and the rhythm on point. Most had never heard anything like it, but supported our joy and energy. We sang some Grandmaster Flash—"Superappin"—and Lady B, "To the Beat Y'all."

We were the center of attention, but to us, we were the only ones in the room. We understood the music; we loved that it was ours. We felt safe for that moment in the midst of uncertainty. This music and that moment were anchors that would help us through what was to come.

Here were two young ladies, telling stories to each other. We were the essence of Hip Hop. This event was the proverbial playground where the genre originated, as we captivated everyone around us. This expression inspired Hip Hop to evolve into a dance style that became yet another way to help like-minded people to embrace each other.

The music and dance have a message: *I see you. You're part of me. I welcome you.*

And that's what happened with me, Maria, and all the people who were enjoying our song.

All good things must come to an end and, after a few hours, our families were allowed to meet with us. That would be the end of my time with Maria in Cuba until our return flight to the States. We shared a tight hug, reminding each other that we were going to be OK and that we would have fun and learn a lot.

"Sing, smile, and breathe," I told her.

She laughed and said, "You, too. Skiddlee beebop."

You know how you get a song in your head, and you can't shake it? Well, "Rapper's Delight" was in my head for 14 days. It was one of the many things I shared from America with my cousins. By the end of my trip, every one of my cousins knew the words and sang it like pros. Do you wonder how they learned an English rap song? Yes they did. You see, it did not matter that they did not know English. What mattered was the beat and emotions that the rhythm gave them. Hip Hop opened the doors for so many other genres, from Rap, Trap, and K-POP, with an international reach that provided the youth the ability to connect through beats.

NIO'S THREE TIPS FOR SURVIVING & THRIVING WITH JOY

I shared my story, along with tips on how to overcome and live joyously, no matter what's happening in your life. Everyone has their own formula, and here is mine. There is no right way to find your joy. It's up to you to be willing and express it in your own unique fierceness. Here is what this slice of life taught me.

Hip Hop provides us with wisdom, and I learned three valuable life lessons from the art form:

- **Have confidence;**

- **Don't become what you hate;** and

- **Stand up for yourself.**

CHAPTER 4

Confidence: when preparation slays fear! You are the power. You have one life and it is up to you to walk your path. Confidence means you own your peace, you are kind, you're able to see the good in others and situations, you walk in curiosity, and you find joy in sharing your talent.

Research has found that self-confidence is the most influential factor in athletic performance. I remember when I used to go to my music competitions and people would ask, "Aren't you nervous?

My answer remained the same from age six to 18: "No, I've practiced and prepared." Those words were key for me, as my mother would ask me every week if I practiced and prepared for my lesson. She wanted to make sure I wasn't wasting her money or time, lugging me across town for lessons.

But what it meant to me was, *Did I own the material to the point that I could close my eyes and play the songs, and do the required exercise as if I had composed them?* Each song had a story in my head, so I could play them with the emotional value they deserved. I thought of the composer and how to do his or her creation justice.

So no, I was not afraid or nervous. I was ready to share the intense passion that I had by being given the opportunity to play the music. It was like that from my first time on stage at age six, playing "Fuer Elise" to an audience of 200 people. It was an honor. Confidence is "When preparedness meets opportunity to share your talents."

Don't Become What You Hate. Standing in your consciousness and balance provides you the ability to stay on track for your dreams, goals, and vision. Hate is an emotion that depletes your energy and diverts you from what is important. Hatred is a learned behavior. We first encounter it in our upbringing through observation and listening to our parents, social and religious limited beliefs about people, politics, norms, and so on. People feel a sense of belonging to be part of a group with similar beliefs. Some people will try to manipulate you into acting a certain way in order to remain accepted in a group.

Often those who have been oppressed, criticized, or abused will inflict similar behavior towards others. This exemplifies the sad reality that "hurt people hurt people." This happens if we are not in full awareness of our actions and understanding that we have full control of our reactions and judgements, then we lean into our subconscious mental chatter.

What is the remedy for this? First and foremost, be kind to yourself, and take the opportunity to shift your perspective and behavior. Hate is in the perception of what you have observed or have come to believe to be true. Shifting your perspective requires being open to accepting those as they are, while embracing the values and decisions that work for you. Know when to stay in your lane and let others live and deal with their decisions.

Stand up for yourself. In Hip Hop, artists historically focused on expressing resiliency and defiance against external threats and laws. The lyrics were about awareness and assertion that:

- You are the change.

- There is nothing you can't do if you put your mind to it and if you focus on hard work.

- You are not limited to the box others place you in, to control you and safeguard their inadequacies.

Be aware that others will try to diminish your light due to their personal fears and insecurities. But you own the brightness of that light; it is a beacon that guides your path and it is your constellation of dreams waiting to erupt with brilliance. Your light helps other through their darkness. When you own your voice, you help others see through the darkness. It is not your job to change others' perceptions, hatred, or limited beliefs. It is your job to bring your undisputed original self to every moment of your life. Live every moment in full consciousness.

CHAPTER 5

Soft Rock & Contemporary Christian – Rebuilt

Soft Rock: a musical genre that is a softened and simplified version of pop rock, originating in Southern California and the United Kingdom during the late 1960s.

Contemporary Christian: Christian Pop is an inspirational genre celebrating the Christian faith. It has roots in Southern Gospel and Gospel music.

Because we put limitations on ourselves, this book is *not* about limitations. The fact of the matter is, when we think of music, it has no boundaries. So, I refuse boundaries.

This chapter is about someone who isn't a female. It's actually about my husband Bob. His name is spelled the same forwards and back. He's a wonderful man who only believes in doing good and is not invested in self-fulfillment. Instead, he's committed to giving to others in a very quiet manner.

The reason I'm talking about Bob in this chapter is because he has a lovely song that has resonated with him his whole life, as he's gone through challenges that can be somewhat unspeakable. His health journey actually goes back to the age of 18 when he was drafted into the military and sent to fight in the Vietnam War. He was captured by the enemy, the Viet Cong.

His extremely cruel captors locked him and other American soldiers in tiger cages, and they were paraded like trophies through villages. Children and adults spat and threw rocks at him and the other soldiers. Bob and the men were beaten daily, while denied hygiene and food. When they were fed, people spit in their food and did other vile things. To this day, my husband has scars on his back where his captors stabbed him and twisted the knives, all for gruesome entertainment, so villagers could cheer as blood poured down his skin. He and his fellow Prisoners of War were treated worse than animals.

Finally, after months of captivity, Bob fought back against one of his captors who came to feed him. He ran away—dodging bullets as his captors shot at him. Nearly naked because his clothes were shredded by the violent abuse, Bob relied on his Eagle Scout training to find his way to safety.

He made it to an American military camp and he was saved. He gave it all for our country, under the guidance of his commanding officer, "Stormin' Norman"—Norman Schwarzkopf, Jr., a kind man and incredible leader. Bob served until he was shipped Statewide for his last four years in the military.

He moved forward in his life. On Thanksgiving Day of 2021, Bob was enjoying a wonderful dinner at a lovely restaurant with me. After my health crisis, we had decided to not travel for the holiday. On our way home as Bob was driving, he said, "I'm having some gastric reflux."

"You ate too much," I said. "Take an antacid when we get home." As we drove, we listened to the first Christmas song of the season—"Santa Baby," beautifully performed by the legendary Eartha Kitt.

At home, that annoying pain continued. He was getting weaker and gray. I needed to call 911, but the last time we

CHAPTER 5

had done that, we were taken to a community hospital that lacked the type of care that he required. So, I stood up and went into action as best I could. I was still walking with a cane in the wake of my hip replacement and bypass surgery. Amazingly, an emergency gives you the adrenaline that you need to move a mountain. Even though my husband is a big guy—6'4" compared to my 5'3" height—I helped him into the car, and I drove like a bat out of hell.

"Please, please don't stop at the lights," he said. "I'll be damned. The pain is getting worse."

He slumped in the car seat.

I was terrified!! His breathing was so shallow, it was almost not happening. I pounded on his chest to make him wake up as I drove.

Tears poured down my face as I blew through stoplights. What would have normally been a 17-minute drive, I drove in nine minutes. With no highway stopping me, I made it to Tufts Medical Center.

I stopped the car at the Washington Street entrance, which is the emergency room. I jumped out of my car, ran inside, and screamed, "Heart attack!"

In seconds, bodies appeared.

"Where?" they asked. "Where? Where?"

"In the car," I said.

They helped him into a wheelchair and he disappeared through the double doors. I went to park the car, then walked into the ER—wearing my badge and walking like I owned the place, even though I was terrified of what was next.

Bob was already being treated in Trauma 2—in the same bay where I had laid fighting for my life only five months earlier. The machines were buzzing. An EKG was attached to him. And a group of doctors and nurses surrounded him as I walked in.

Dr. Chin saw me and said, "Look at this." He showed me an EKG.

"This is serious," I said.

They assumed he had two blocked arteries. His blood pressure was through the roof. They immediately took him to the Cath lab. I tried to keep up as they rushed him up to the procedure room.

"Go to the Cath Lab waiting room," one of the nurses said.

I wasn't having that. I sat on the floor outside of the procedure room. I wanted to hear everything. It was late and the hospital was empty, as it was the holiday, so no one moved me. There I was, sitting outside the lab door, praying, and supplicating, hoping my lovely husband would be OK. I could hear the conversation in the lab as they were doing his surgery. True to Bob, he was awake, cracking jokes, as humor is one of his favorite reactions to adversity.

"You know," he told the OR team, "it's all about perspective. For a healthy man, I'm sick. For a dying man, I'm blessed." That quote from comedian Flip Wilson is one of Bob's favorites.

Then he went into his usual quirky jokes that usually only resonate who people who share his quirky mental compass. Bob makes a joke about everything.

"Doc," he said, "Can we change the tunes in the procedure room? Let's have a dance party!"

Bob does not dance, but he sure was making everyone laugh while he laughed along with them. **They were saving his life.**

Tears poured down my face in gratitude to God for giving the doctors the talent to save him, and for keeping him in good spirits. I heard footsteps coming towards the door, so I rolled out of the way and tried to stand up as fast as possible. When the door swung open, Dr. Chin was smiling.

"He did great," Dr. Chin said. "By the way, he is hilarious! We put in two stents. He is going to be fine!"

Why did I begin with the story about Vietnam? And how does it come full circle?

CHAPTER 5

Sadly, Bob's story illustrates the dysfunction and unfairness of our health care system. When he enlisted in the U.S. Army, he was told that he would get Veterans Administration health benefits for the rest of his life. After his service, and the trauma of being a POW, he certainly believed that he had earned that. Plus, he was decorated with two silver star medals among others and received an honorable discharge.

Yet when he contacted the VA to receive his health benefits, he received no confirmation. Instead, his weekly phone calls were transferred from one department to another with no answers.

Then, after I became self-employed, our health insurance game changed, and Bob thought he could tap into his VA coverage. Wrong. He was informed that the USA had determined that the Viet Cong was not a legitimate military force. So basically, Bob's military career is null; his Vietnam experience doesn't exist. His scars, pain, and memories are no longer acknowledged by the Army. Adding insult to the situation, they detailed his whole career and called it irrelevant.

"Your benefits under that statue are not guaranteed," he was told. "Maybe the fact that you were exposed to Agent Orange may qualify benefits. As a victim of Agent Orange, we will check."

We're still waiting on an answer and final decision.

The day my husband heard those words was the first time he truly felt sadness and opened up to me about his time in the military.

"I am no victim," Bob had decided after being captured.

He was going to move on with his life he would never forget, but he would not be stuck in memories. He was going to live his present moments. Ordinarily, he doesn't talk about his time in the military; he's a silent giant in giving and caring. But now there he was, sitting in our dining room, telling me:

"This has been the greatest rejection. After all these

years, this should not be the case for any of our veterans. I gave freely with n expectation of glory. But I do think that I should be respected enough to get a determination as to my healthcare eligibility."

We sat in silence for a while. He stood up and started humming his song. The song that freed mind. When sorrow and hardship were all around him, as an 18-year-old in Vietnam, the tune in his head carried him through. This was a source of never-ending comfort, an enabler of peace in his heart. It made him free and able to move forward.

The songs, those wonderful songs, oh, they were many. But there were some that were special, three in the account, a mix of Soft Rock and Roll and Contemporary Christian music. Can you imagine an 18-year-old going through such major trauma in his life? And having to cling to some songs to persevere and help him thrive against all odds? These are the three magical rock and roll songs that gave him the strength:

- **"Gimme Shelter featuring Lisa Fischer" by The Rolling Stones**. This beautiful version provides stability during tough times. It's something to laugh at, yet it's very telling.
- **"Keep Your Hands to Yourself" by Georgia Satellites.**
- **"Scars in Heaven" by Casting Crowns.**

These three special songs in the categories of Rock and Roll and Christian Contemporary, each marking different life chapters, all made a difference. These songs can move a person forward in the midst of adversity; that's why Bob hums "**Gimme Shelter**" during those moments when he needs strength.

We have so many moments where we are denied in life, but denial does not mean that you are frozen. It just means you look for a different path and a new perspective. You just change your tune to adjust to the situation. This trait helps great people move forward and find their way.

"No one denies you," Bob told me. "You deny yourself. Learn from the fact that you have the power to act." This message echoes the lyrics in **"Keep Your Hands to Yourself."**

You must set your boundaries and define what is acceptable or not in your life. Everyone will love you if you do their will, but respect happens when you have clearly defined boundaries and an understanding of your power. When the power seems to be taken away from you, it's just a moment in time that your lens lost its focus on your set boundaries. It merely is a glimpse of someone else's perspective on you. You don't have to embrace it. You just need to fight on, going forward. Make it through the pain. Make it when no one else expects you to make it. Thank you, Bob, for giving me the song in your heart.

The last song is a newcomer. **"Scars in Heaven"** is special because it touched our hearts at such a critical time in our lives. It was a refuge when both Bob and I were both at death's door in 2021. When losing each other became a grim possibility, all within one year, Bob selected **"Scars in Heaven."** This beautiful Christian rock song talks about that moment when you realize that the one person you found, the one who makes your life better, the person you love, may be gone. The song reminds us that the spirit still shines through the scars.

"Scars in Heaven" gave us the words we didn't have to communicate our feelings and how our love and faith centered us. This happened when he saw me—and I was not awake—in a bright white ICU room full of machines to keep me alive. Bob held my hand; he smelled the antiseptic used to sterilize the room to prevent infection. Our life was forever changed, and **"Scars in Heaven"** brought solace. It reminded Bob that he has control over his commitment and loving relationship with God. You can control your actions, beliefs, and energy, but not anything external that happens to a loved one.

He struggled with letting go of what would become my future, and placing my fate in God's hands. Thanks be to God that I came back to him. Meanwhile, my health crisis propelled Bob on a journey of remembering his father, as well as his mother and many family members, friends, and Army buddies, who had passed before with no warning. He stared at the chronicles of life, knowing that those scars, those beautiful people who left us in pain, are thriving in heaven. And he's blessed to have had them.

We can't control what's going to happen. But we can rejoice in the present. We can make sure that we do one simple thing: outdo each other's niceness. When someone does something nice for you, make it a point to do something nicer for them. Because when the moments of scars in heaven happened, you will have the opportunity to rest on those moments of "nice"—giving to each other an experience worth putting a smile on our faces, sharing those moments of joy, and cherishing those moments of giving and exchanging for each other without any conditions, in complete abandonment.

Let's rejoice and understand that we can't control things, while knowing that God is in control and provides us our beacon of light that is continuous joy. And it's all together about leading with kindness.

PHOTO GALLERY

Gloria Gaynor singing an original song at my wedding.

Antonio (Tony) and Mireya Queiro on January 31, 1959. The Queiro Family was formed.

JOY NOTES

Mireya and Tony Queiro in 2022. I am, because they were my guides.

That special performance when you win "best in your age group" for classical piano and you receive a standing ovation for your first dance solo.

PHOTO GALLERY

*Kayaking at Kripalu Center For Yoga & Health,
September 2021.
When you find your inner strength to restore
your mind, body, and spirit.*

*Lora Carr saving me when I lost my way.
Thanks for being my friend.*

JOY NOTES

My love and me. Bob and Nio.

Father's Day 2022 with the Queiro Family: Bob, Papi (Tony), Mami (Mireya), Michelle, Cylas, Quinton, Kyle, Cameron, Henry. This was my Dad's last Father's Day.

Quinton, Cylas, and Michelle— my children and grandson, my most precious gift from God.

CHAPTER 6

Jazz—Improvise

Jazz: a music genre originating in African American communities in New Orleans, Louisiana, during the late 1800s and early 1900s. Rooted in blues and ragtime, it features swing and blue notes, complex chords, call and response vocals, polyrhythms **and** improvisation.

Jazz is the music of improvisation, syncopation, and wild rhythm. It is the music of nature that lets us fly like an eagle with reservation. Jazz opened the door for Black Americans to express themselves in the midst of pain, drama, despair, joy, and resurgence. It opens the door to freedom and giving others their voice through music. Jazz is the only music genre that has never been predefined and it is applauded when it starts with a base and then flies into free expression.

Many say that music is the voice of life. This is especially true in Jazz, because no matter the situation, it demonstrates resiliency and perseverance. It provides the individual's narrative and takes you from the pain to joy.

So how is this important to you? What can you learn from Jazz? And why care?

JOY NOTES

I remember finding myself lost in a job that was portrayed as a dream opportunity during the interview process. I was elated to join this organization. Unfortunately, during the first week's onboarding, I realized this was a case of smoke and mirrors. I had left a good organization and a supportive boss, to seek the next rung up the career ladder, but the ladder was leaning against the wrong wall. Likewise, the environment did not align with my values and professional standards.

What do you do in a situation like this? Well, you go through three stages of grief. These are the same stages that we endure after a debilitating illness is diagnosed in ourselves or a love done.

During the first stage of grief, you ask yourself, "Why? Why me? Why did I miss the signs? Why now?" Then the self and external analysis happen. We search to understand ourselves and everything regarding the situation and condition. We become so well versed, that we fall into the second stage.

The second stage is depression, sadness, and anger. We feel broken, full of stress and tension. We become still in the situation, trying to find our emotions. In this stillness, we eventually understand that this is what we have to deal with. We open ourselves to using it as a learning experience, and find the power within to transform it into something of value.

Jazz music takes us through the path of this journey. It starts quietly, providing awareness, and then it goes into a low, steady rhythm, ticking away till the next stage.

The third stage is when we exhale and immerse in thankfulness. We hear the music swell and blossom in triumph. As humans, whether we are talking about illness or professional madness, this is when you are praising that you woke up that morning and that you have a new day to make new decisions. You understand that there are no mistakes and you are in this moment for a reason.

CHAPTER 6

Jazz is also celebrated for providing the magic of improvisation, which means being creative in the moment, following your intuition, and creating a whole new way of thinking and behaving in a situation. While improvised Jazz vocals and music during a live performance are extremely entertaining and enchanting, the application of improvisation to difficult circumstances can be just as transformative and uplifting.

In my story about taking the wrong job, my improvisation in less than ideal circumstances inspired me to focus on delivering my best work and helping those around me who were struggling succeed. I was able to make the time purposeful and I am grateful for all that I learned. I have greater skills for dealing with people who are fueled by fear, survival, and greed.

When you're in the midst of trouble, you do not have to be affected by what is occurring outside of you. You must center yourself and focus on the issues that directly affect you. This will require managing your energy and emotions and not being consumed by the mayhem surrounding you.

In that job, people tried to share gossip with me. Just like when you may cover your ears to block out a song that you don't like, or that reminds of you of lost love or a difficult period of your life, I would immediately change the conversation and disengage from the negative energy. I understood that my responsibility was to elevate the energy in the room and inside of me. My positivity and capability to overcome empowered me as I embraced the ability to accept that which I could not control, and instead focused my energy on that which I can influence and deliver. In illness, you learn to guard your heart. You fill yourself with an optimistic focus on the possibilities and open your mind to joy. You melt the anger, depression, and bitterness into a passage of change.

I eventually left the position for a better opportunity, but I gained so many friends and learnings that have fortified me as a better leader and person, that I cherish that time in my life.

Jazz was a great comfort and instrument that helped me improvise new ways of coping with and resolving challenges. I don't know your personal belief in a greater power, but what I do know is that across our religions and ideologies, music and praise are essential for the unification of the basic ideals of life. When a person is dying, one of the last senses to fail is the ability to hear. Many have said that is because this phase is a chance to enter the final phase of the life cycle in melodic praise.

Pastor Tania Fuentes Epitomizes the Power of Jazz to Heal and Transform

We are now going to continue with interviews in this and the later chapters. I conducted these interviews with phenomenal women across the country. Their stories about health, healing, and the power of music can provide powerful lessons for you to apply to your life.

Each woman has found her *Joy Notes* and uses her unique platform to share them with people who need them most.

These interviews that are presented in a Q&A format each epitomize a musical genre and explore how each woman—as well as my father and my husband—find their *Joy Notes* in life, and how you can, too.

In particular, **Pastor Tania Fuentes** is the Senior Pastor of the Love of Jesus Family Church of West New York. For more than 30 years, she has been sharing the goodness of God.

We met in a carpool with our kids, who were attending the same private school. While we were standing at the school, waiting for the kids to be let out, she told me about her church and we realized we knew some of the same people. After that, I began attending her church, where the pastor was her husband and she was the First Lady.

CHAPTER 6

From the moment we met, Pastor Tania exuded an energy of kindness that I had never witnessed before. I had never met a person who lit up a room like the sun while being kind to everyone. It wasn't fake; this was her authentic nature. To meet a woman who looked like me and radiated so much love, I naturally gravitated to her.

Pastor Tania and the women I interviewed in this book each struck me in a beautiful way that I can only describe as excellence and a blessing of lasting, meaningful friendship.

Now I have the privilege and pleasure of sharing their stories and their wisdom with you. Enjoy and glean nuggets of wisdom that help you find your *Joy Notes*.

Nio: Pastor Tania, thank you for your time to talk about *Joy Notes: From Balancing Trauma to Triumph.*

The book is about the harrowing things that women go through in healthcare and how we have our trauma, and we have to maneuver it through life.

How did you move forward?

What can you tell other women?

And how did music empower you?

There's a song that God puts in our hearts during our trauma, and that's the conversation. Now I'm opening the door for you to tell one of your stories.

Pastor Tania: If you've had the privilege of having a child, that in itself is traumatic, especially the first time when you're not as educated or experienced in this. I can go through different stages, but early in my life . . . for my first child, I had no idea what to expect. And [in the hospital] when I heard other women screaming, they were screaming out of terror, out of fear, and I could hear them. Something happened within me; I was paralyzed. I told the doctors and . . . nurses there, "I don't want to give birth!"

Now, I'm on the birthing bed, I was mortified. I got up from there, and I started literally running. They had to hold me; they had to strap me. And . . . I almost lost my life.

Nio: Could you explain a little bit more of how you almost lost your life?

Pastor Tania: The mental impact that I experienced during this situation, the trauma, left a mark in me. First of all, being strapped so I could be held down. I think it was like 18 hours before I finally gave birth. But I was so terrified that it was no longer the situation that I was going through— it was a trauma of hearing other women screaming. And I vowed to myself:

No matter whatever happens in my life, I will learn to quiet those screams, because fear and trauma will bring depression, will bring hopelessness, will bring fear.

So there was a song during that time; it became very personal to me and it dealt with the love of God.

It just dealt with the unfailing love of God, which never ceases us, never stops. They are new every morning. And I had to start basking in that. I had to condition myself with the help of God to come to a place where I can say, "God, I know that you love me."

I know that the traumatic things that I've heard . . . those screaming women, when I felt helpless and hopeless, I couldn't even go and help them because I was going through my own trauma. But suddenly that song, it became an anthem for me for many years. You are unfailing; love never ceases. And it's amazing because that song comes from the scripture of Lamentations 3:22-23 ESV:

"The steadfast love of the LORD never ceases; his mercies never come to an end; they are new every morning; great is your faithfulness."

And the funny thing is that in the midst of your lamenting, in the midst of a trial, in the midst of a challenge, in the midst

CHAPTER 6

of loneliness, here is this prophet talking about the unfailing love of God. And so that has carried me throughout the years.

Later on in the years, I lost two of my children, but I was able to hold on to the unfailing love of God. It's a Gospel song. And it worked in me by providing hope. And I have been able to impart this hope to other young women who suffer from postpartum depression, who have been abused during pregnancy, and who have thought less of themselves. I'm talking about women who are professional, that because of that one act, they have kept their mouth quiet. And I tell them:

"You no longer have to be quiet. There's someone who loves you. You need to start loving yourself, because this is how God sees you in spite of what you've gone through."

With me, I was only 20 years old at that time, but that song carried me through every single situation that I faced in my life.

Nio: That's interesting. We were basically the same age. Same thing, I was 20 years old when I had Quintin. So, I know what you're saying. And here you are, a preacher's wife. Your husband [the late Pastor Mickey Fuentes who passed in 2005] was a pastor.

Pastor Tania: Yes.

Nio: And you're a pastor now. And yet the reality is, there's that situation that you can't explain, that takes so much out of you, right?

Pastor Tania: Oh, yes, I could have become a victim, but I'm so grateful. And then throughout the years, that song resonates, even today. It resonates in the challenges. It has helped to shape and mold me in situations that I know where I could not have done it on my own. I understand the very presence of God. For me, it's not a religion. For me, it's not a dogma theory, but it's a reality. I live a reality. And I've seen, because of that, the transformation in other women's lives, and it's empowering; it's enriching to be able to give to others. And you writing this book, I believe that is something powerful. It's like becoming the voice to the voiceless.

And that in itself, it causes you to say, I have a purpose. I have a destiny. And no matter where I come from, what background I come from, I know that I am loved. We usually love so many people, but the Bible is so clear when it says you have to love your neighbor as you love yourself. And a lot of people love the neighbors and they don't love themselves because they feel that they are not lovely, that they are not who others perceive them to be, or actually how you think other people perceive you. Again, this journey of being in situations that could have been destructive, but it's like when you go to a gym and you work out and you start to develop muscles; the strength comes through the pain of exercising.

But this work is not in vain. It produces strength, it produces courage, it produces vision—it actually produces vision. Just like you writing this book, it's a vision that has come from the things I'm sure that you have lived and you have seen and you have come through. You said, "I'm going to push through."

And I believe that that's one of the things that is in us as women, especially women of color, women who are my background, Latina, where sometimes society might reject who you are—

Nio: And completely underestimate you.

Pastor Tania: Yes, exactly. And they say, "What? You have a college degree? What? You are a CEO of a company? What?

You have your own business? They absolutely underestimate you. And when they see the progress in your life, when they see that you have excelled, how was it that you did it?"

Nio: Yes.

Pastor Tania: Guess what, I tell other women, you can do it, too. You can dream.

Nio: I'll never forget the first time I was on a business trip and I said, "Oh, I grew up in West New York, New Jersey," to a person who was also a Jersey native.
   And she says, "Oh, isn't that where all the workers are? The cleaning ladies? The lawn people? Isn't that where they come from?"

Pastor Tania: Wow.

Nio: I was like, "I'm your boss."

Pastor Tania: My God.

Nio: And I told her, "You are basically taking everybody who lives in my little town and we cannot be anything more, which there's no shame in it because, as far as I'm concerned, a dollar earned with hard work is a valuable dollar. How dare you put me in a category that makes you feel better!"

Pastor Tania: Exactly. Wow. That is really serious business. But guess what? Your person speaks volumes. Your person validates you. You know what I'm saying? And that again, song that validates you that you hold on to. With me, I like Jazz, but I hold on to Gospel music. Not every Gospel song, but there are certain songs that remind us that His love never ceases us. It just resonates within me. And when sometimes you might feel loveless because of the situation you're going through, you might think, *Lord, I worked so hard for this and it seems like it's not going to happen.*

But with me, it just pushes me to go further, to push forward, not backwards. And if I should happen to slip backwards, that gives me the power to go right back.

Nio: Never look back, not even for the push forward. That's the Cuban way that we've learned our whole life.

Pastor Tania: Yes, absolutely. Also, there's an old song that Andraé Crouch would sing 20 years ago. And that also filled me with hope. The Bible says, hope does not make you ashamed. Some people think that hoping is something that is not strong, but when you hope in God, you cannot help but be what He says—be more than a conqueror. If it had not been for the Lord, where would I be?

Nio: I'm so glad you said that. I'm so tired of people being so negative about hope. Hope has turned into a dirty word.

Pastor Tania: Yes.

Nio: And how did that happen? With hope, we got power. Hope gave us the strength to move forward when we couldn't have any more energy. The hope helped us move forward. And now people talk about how hope without a plan, is nothing. How does that happen? How did we lose hope?

Pastor Tania: This brings to recollection the great Psalm, and a great singer, David. And David suffered from depression. He had money and influence. But he started declaring over himself—and this is something that I practice most

CHAPTER 6

times—asking myself:

"Why are you depressed, oh my soul?"

In other words, **realign yourself**. Why are you depressed? And then [David] says something powerful; he says, **hope in God**. Hope in God, because I'm still going to worship Him, or I'm still going to sing. I am still going to acknowledge Him, but it's going to be through song. And the word universe, God created the universe. That word universe in its original form is the word, one song. So even the universe, God, in His great wisdom, He created the universe. David said He created it with a song, one song, one song. So it's just that one song that will get you through. The creator of the heavens and the Earth of the universe, created everything through a song. And even the scripture says that he sings over.

So, if no one else is singing praises unto you, if no one else is acknowledging you, like when I was in that hospital bed, the only one who I knew who would sing over me was the living God. So, universe, universe, universe. One song, one song, he says, all you need is one song. And if no one is singing over you, I'm doing it. Hallelujah. Praise the Lord.

Nio: Praise the Lord. That's so powerful. I had no idea when I had woken up from my two cardiac arrests and going through so much in June of 2021, and I said, "Lord, why?"

And everybody thinks the why was, "Why did it happen?"

No, that wasn't my why. My why was, "Why am I here? What is the purpose you have for me?" And it kept saying:

"Tell the story. Tell the story, bring me the glory. And don't tell only your story, bring others."

And this book is a labor of love, of giving back voice to women who don't have a voice that tells themselves every single day, "Why, why, why?"

But I knew that what helped me was the song in my heart. And now I understand that that's the universe. Now the link is complete. And that's why I said, *No, the book has to be about the song in the heart through the trauma.* Because every single woman that I've spoken to has given me a song.

Pastor Tania: Praise God.

Nio: That is just an affirmation of the Lord saying, "The universe is one song."

Pastor Tania: My God. Oh, that's awesome. Praise God. You're talking about your experience in 2021. Well, I went through COVID, but this was actually after COVID that I got it. I didn't know how sick I was and I was taken to the hospital in that emergency room. Again, the songs kept coming to me about hope. And I looked around and I could say, "You're in the emergency room."

And God said, in the midst of that, "I want you to look around and I want you to pray because there are people here who are hopeless, but you are not."

In that stage, I looked around and thought I was in pain, though I didn't know that I had pneumonia. Later on, I found out that the doctor had said, "It's a miracle that you're alive after being hospitalized for almost a week."

As they were rolling me away to a bedroom, I saw this elderly person laying in that bed. And I looked into his eyes and I prayed within me, but I smiled at him. And I know that there was a connection, because I saw this person, hopeless. But the song within me, again, from the universe, from that one song that God sang, I know that it empowered. I know that this person said, "I'm not alone."

But two weeks after I was discharged, younger people told me: "You didn't survive, but you went through. And every nurse, every physician that wouldn't go into my room . . . there's something different about it."

And I would say, "It's not something, it's someone.

Because of what you radiate and that song caused you to radiate the reality of who [God] is in your life when you are going through that trauma."

For me, that was music, especially from my Latino background, because my mom educated me in different songs of different genres.

As a result, I said, "I never had a habit." My habit was music, a song, a dance, a tango, depending on where I was or what I was experiencing. It was that song. It could be opera, I love opera. So you don't understand it. But I said, "Yeah, there's an articulation in music that you don't have to say words, even though you don't understand the language, the articulation of music starts to resonate within you."

And even your body reacts to it. Notice that a lot of people who might be walking through depression, they don't want to hear anything. They want to stay shut in. And if they hear anything, it's songs that bring you down. But there's something about praise and worship that brings hope. And it enlightens you, it empowers you, my God. And then all of a sudden, you look back, you say, "Wow, look what the Lord has done!"

That's what He says that He inhabits. He makes a habitation of the praises of His people. And a praise, it doesn't have to be in a choir; it could just be saying, "Thank you, Lord, for another beautiful day." And you could sing a 'Thank you, Lord' for another powerful day. And then He inhabits that and you become part of that universe, that one song that He sings over you. So again, I am thrilled as to the inspiration that God has given you to write this, to express this, to share this. It is phenomenal. And I'm very happy and proud of you that you have responded to the call.

Nio: Thank you. I am, every day, blessed. He told me who to talk to through the book. It's been truly in prayer. And He gave me the names.

JOY NOTES

Pastor Tania: Oh, my God.

Nio: I have gone through an experience that has been so spiritual. It has literally changed me, because I go to the rock for everything.

Pastor Tania: Praise God.

Nio: And it's just a feeling of, *there is no fear.* I walked away from my job to build my own thing. And I know that this act is an act of praise to God.

Pastor Tania: Amen. That's right. Absolutely. And you know what, the beauty of this is, you and I can never out-give God.

Nio: Never, ever.

Pastor Tania: As you give this inspiration, He's going to give you so much more because there's more in you. This is awesome. Like I said, when I say I'm proud of you, I did not know the extent of the experience that you're having, but you don't have to say too much, because it emanates from you.

So, like I said, I'm excited. I am thrilled because you have allowed yourself to be that vessel of honor, bringing honor to Him. And like I said, since you cannot out-give Him, He gives you honor. He gets the glory; you get the honor.

The fact that you said, "I wanted other people to share, I wanted other women to share in this," He said, "That's the heart of God because Jesus will have come and done everything on His own."

But He said, "I need 12 dysfunctional men so I can make them function, so I can impart to them, so I can give to them what I have."

And that's what you are doing, that's what you have,

you're giving to others, and that is something that is very rare in these times that we're living. So, congratulations.

Nio: Thank you, Mama. I appreciate you. I miss you, I miss your praise. I miss being in your church.

PASTOR TANIA'S THREE TIPS FOR SURVIVING & THRIVING WITH JOY

Pastor Tania provided a look into her moments of trauma and triumph, and shares tips on how to persevere and embrace the goodness in life, especially during pain and tragedy.

Here are her three suggestions for hitting the *Joy Notes* in your life:

1. **Acknowledge the power of God through song.** When Pastor Tania was enduring the nightmarish screaming of other women giving birth, and at the same time being strapped down to a hospital bed during her own 18-hour labor, then trying to heal from the trauma of that doubly troubling experience, she acknowledged God's healing power through music. She listened to a favorite gospel song that lifted her from the depths of despair into the peace. God's song also empowered her to help other women do the same.

2. **Realign yourself with hope.** Pastor Tania finds no shame in hope, which like faith, is the evidence of things not seen. Believing is knowing that God will always pull you through, with the best possible outcome, in divine timing.

Hope is the tool that serves as a catalyst to transform pain, sadness, and fear into uplifting emotions that enable survival and healing. Hope also opens a channel of divine communicate, so that you're able to hear God's guidance, such as when He told her to look at those in the ER when she had COVID and appreciate that she had strength from hope, whereas others lacked that soothing and even life-saving power.

3. **Play the music!** When Pastor Tania has struggled, she plays her favorite uplifting songs. The lyrics, the melodies, the rhythms, all have a magical ability to delight the senses and activate spiritual power within and around you, to lift the angst, the pain, the sadness, and elevate you into a mindset and physical feeling of relief and even optimism. To do this, you need to identify which songs have this power for you. Then hold nothing back. Play the song or songs over and over in your headphones, on your car stereo, on your phone, on your sound system. Put the song on repeat and immerse in the sound bath to cleanse and clear any negative energy. Hum softly or sing along with the lyrics at the top of your lungs. Dance. Blast the music. And don't turn it off until you feel better.

You can learn more about Pastor Tania at her website: https://www.loveofjesuswny.com/our-pastor-2

CHAPTER 7

Country—Tell It Like It is, with Raw Honesty

*C*ountry: a musical genre deeply rooted deeply in Black culture as a genre that was brought to America from the African enslaved people with their banjos and use of music for storytelling. The Negro spirituals created the foundation for country, blues and folk music.

Raw Honesty is a powerful force. As a woman, we experience it during those moments when you take a deep look at yourself in the mirror, without the filters that make us comfortable. When we drop the excuses and the rationalizations, then we can deal with ourselves. We can see what is important and what are our roles, paths, and opportunities.

Country Music is all about Raw Honesty. The lyrics and melodies often focus on sad love stories, melancholy tales about life and loss, the happy times anchored by the disappointments of life, and so much more. The twangy tunes of Country Music keeps it real. It doesn't sugar-coat life, love, or self. It takes a raw look at pain, struggle, and sacrifice. This genre teaches us powerful lessons to apply

Raw Honesty to ourselves, our relationships, our work, our health, and our life experiences.

Raw Honesty has been a powerful dynamic in my life. As I look back to my experiences, I think of that time at Kripalu when I took off the face paint, designer clothes, and the safety mask. This was a time that I walked into simplicity, opened to my vulnerability, and gave myself RESPECT. I respected my pain and acknowledged my needs. Opening the door to my raw truth, I learned that messes take time to clean up and I needed to fight to restore myself.

As you embrace your Raw HONESTY, you find yourself able to breathe, in a state of now. Ask yourself, "What do I need to move forward?" Here are some suggestions:

- Make a commitment to yourself to be honest with yourself.
- Acknowledge that you need time to restore.
- Make self-reflection part of your everyday life.
- Speak your intentions out loud.
- Don't feel guilty about caring for your mind, body, and spirit. It's **your** life.

A woman who exemplifies the power of Raw Honesty with the same realness as Country Music is **Dr. Adrianne Johnson Ross.** She is a true renaissance woman, able to recreate herself multiple times while using her many talents towards her purpose. She has a Bachelor's Degree in Organizational Psychology from Georgia State University, a Master's in Healthcare Administration from George Washington University and a PhD in Healthcare Business Administration from the Medical University of South Carolina.

Adrianne is the former President and COO of the University of Vermont Health Network, Home Health & Hospice organization.

CHAPTER 7

Country—Tell It Like It is, with Raw Honesty

*C*ountry: a musical genre deeply rooted deeply in Black culture as a genre that was brought to America from the African enslaved people with their banjos and use of music for storytelling. The Negro spirituals created the foundation for country, blues and folk music.

Raw Honesty is a powerful force. As a woman, we experience it during those moments when you take a deep look at yourself in the mirror, without the filters that make us comfortable. When we drop the excuses and the rationalizations, then we can deal with ourselves. We can see what is important and what are our roles, paths, and opportunities.

Country Music is all about Raw Honesty. The lyrics and melodies often focus on sad love stories, melancholy tales about life and loss, the happy times anchored by the disappointments of life, and so much more. The twangy tunes of Country Music keeps it real. It doesn't sugar-coat life, love, or self. It takes a raw look at pain, struggle, and sacrifice. This genre teaches us powerful lessons to apply

Raw Honesty to ourselves, our relationships, our work, our health, and our life experiences.

Raw Honesty has been a powerful dynamic in my life. As I look back to my experiences, I think of that time at Kripalu when I took off the face paint, designer clothes, and the safety mask. This was a time that I walked into simplicity, opened to my vulnerability, and gave myself RESPECT. I respected my pain and acknowledged my needs. Opening the door to my raw truth, I learned that messes take time to clean up and I needed to fight to restore myself.

As you embrace your Raw HONESTY, you find yourself able to breathe, in a state of now. Ask yourself, "What do I need to move forward?" Here are some suggestions:

- Make a commitment to yourself to be honest with yourself.
- Acknowledge that you need time to restore.
- Make self-reflection part of your everyday life.
- Speak your intentions out loud.
- Don't feel guilty about caring for your mind, body, and spirit. It's **your** life.

A woman who exemplifies the power of Raw Honesty with the same realness as Country Music is **Dr. Adrianne Johnson Ross.** She is a true renaissance woman, able to recreate herself multiple times while using her many talents towards her purpose. She has a Bachelor's Degree in Organizational Psychology from Georgia State University, a Master's in Healthcare Administration from George Washington University and a PhD in Healthcare Business Administration from the Medical University of South Carolina.

Adrianne is the former President and COO of the University of Vermont Health Network, Home Health & Hospice organization.

CHAPTER 7

We met through work, but bonded over our passion to assist the underserved and our dedication to educating children from diverse backgrounds, to help them fulfill their goals and dreams. We worked together and supported multiple 501c3 efforts.

She also has a long musical career as a singer, composer, songwriter, and collaborator with many of the current R&B celebrities who are in vogue.

I asked Adrianne to tell her personal story, because it was so true to the issues that women of color experience in maternal care and post-delivery care. She and her children are survivors of a failed system of care delivery.

Adrianne's story involves self-reflection, embracing self, and confronting your internal and external truths. Adrianne fought for her life when she was rejected time and time again—personally during her health battle, and professionally in the boardroom. Standing on honesty and paying attention to self, she was able to keep moving in her path to joy.

During the trauma of being on the verge of losing her life, Adrienne fought to live and to preserve her identity. Her triumph comes from understanding that you must live every moment and not hide behind the mask that makes you comfortable. This is the mask that keeps you safe from having to acknowledge your emotions and the impact that external facts are having on you.

Often, we do everything to stay invisible. There is no triumph until you embrace your truths. They may not be pretty at times, but there is nothing to fear. You can make it through. You are valuable, worthy, and powerful. You have to stand for your unique beautiful truth and for what is right.

During her struggles, Adrienne found comfort in music, especially in the Folk Rock/Soft Rock/Pop song "You Got A Friend" by James Taylor released in 1971. This song is a source of hope and an affirmation that you can be accepted as you are, without your mask. There are wonderful people who support and love us as our whole selves.

At the same time, Adrianne is perfect for Country, because she is all about Raw Truth, because she told me during our interview that, "The most important thing is to know your truth and deal with yourself."

Women, especially Black women, tend to dress up, apply makeup, get our hair and nails done, and place great importance on our appearance, because we want acceptance. Unfortunately, as we create this façade that we present to the world, sometimes we forget to look in the mirror with Raw Honesty.

In the following interview, Dr. Adrianna Johnson Ross shows us how to do that.

Niobis Queiro: Let's talks about trauma and tragedy in your life's journey. You've had many and came out triumphant.

Adrianna Johnson Ross: As an African American female growing up in the South, being educated in the United States system, and kind of cutting my teeth . . . in healthcare, I began to soon realize not so much on the academic side, but once I began to work professionally, that I was different.

I began to understand that when I was just simply doing my job, it was received differently than when others did their job. So my story involves multiple situations on the administrative side, which includes partners, hospital, ambulatory, what have you, and basic leadership, holding others accountable, being responsible, being self-aware of whatever the goals were of the organization.

One would think that if you are clear and have these as our goals, we're going from a current state to a future state, that building the bridge in between would be enough, as long as you bring everyone along with you. But maturing is a part of that, an understanding that you have to bring leadership along with you as well. So, I was not accustomed to being a target, but I learned very quickly that being an African American woman, you are quickly a target when you are doing well.

CHAPTER 7

Nio: I really want to hear more about this, because there's a trauma in that, right, in knowing that you're different? How did that impact you? Yet you didn't surrender to it? How have you pushed through that situation?

Adrianne: Going deeper, deeper into my self-awareness has taken a tremendous amount of time and therapy. It has been a tremendous self-journey. A tremendous amount of time delving into myself historically, by going back into childhood, learning more about self-discovery! I had to learn what are my own issues and limitations before I could recognize how I was showing up in a health system with others.

Nio: That's the fact. If you don't know you, then you can't even show up completely. No.

Adrianne: Can't do it.

Nio: So, that makes total sense. Now, I know that you've been through a lot, even beyond your leadership journey, which you know, we had the joy of being able to work together, and that was a true partnership and I'm blessed that I had that opportunity. But I remember when I first met you and we broke bread. And we were talking about the trauma in healthcare as Black women, and you shared with me a story of you being near death, and how you were able to maneuver that situation. And look at the person you are now.

   I think that story is so worth sharing, because nobody would. Normally, you see, people would live in self-pity. But you didn't. You came out victorious. Could you share that story?

Adrianne: Sure can. It was the summer of 2000 and I was pregnant with Dennis, my son. I was having tremendous abdominal pain. I was living in Atlanta, Georgia, at the time.

I went to the hospital, and I had on my wedding band. These are standard protocols for a woman of color because of the stereotypes. You don't want to be seen as a baby mama, one on food stamps, sucking resources from the system. The physician on the registration can see what type of insurance you have, and whether it's government insurance, or a commercial payer.

So, being a part of the system myself as an administrator, **I had a front-row seat to racism, discrimination, bias,** day in and day out, so I knew how I had to be dressed. How I dress impacts how I'm treated.

But I was very, very ill that day. Ambulance came, picked me up. I was toxic so far as toxicity levels, very sick, very ill . . . so I was not able to speak and was falling unconscious. The ambulance took me to the hospital, but the ER turned me away, ultimately, four times.

The first time, I heard **the nurse saying, "Oh, she's probably drug-seeking."** I heard that, I heard her words. I was on a gurney in the hallway. I can hear it now, and I felt my body go down. I felt my body relax in a disappointing way, because I knew that that was going to impact the rest of my care. From those words forward, I was turned away from the hospital again. Ultimately, an additional three more times. I went back the fourth time with a friend.

Nio: So they turned you away, even though you came in an ambulance, and that you are unconscious, and they turned you away as a drug seeker?

Adrianne: Yes. So, they brought me back home. I am very vague on what happened after that. I had my son with me. I was breast feeding him. I remember trying to call my parents. I couldn't speak well. I couldn't remember phone numbers. Another ambulance from the fire department came. I remember leaving again, and my son was with two

CHAPTER 7

firemen, and they had him in their arms.

I left again. Yes, I left with another ambulance. At that point, the same thing happened again. I remember hearing, again, words like that. They sent me home again. I was waiting in the lobby for a taxi to take me home this time. The pain was so bad. I got on the floor in the waiting room, and **I remember a nurse coming out, saying, "You can't be on the floor in here."**

Then I said, "I cannot sit in a chair." I just was kind of mumbling that, it wasn't clear, it wasn't articulate, but that wasn't gonna happen. So, I was just **writhing in pain** and got sent home again. And then another ambulance came a third time.

Nio: Is there anyone? Is there a phone number?

Adrianne: Somehow, miraculously, the only number I could think of was an old friend, Karas. They called her. She came over with her husband. She had just walked in the door from her honeymoon. Her husband found an itinerary behind the fax machine and was able to call my husband. Karas took me home with her. It was horrible, but she, again, took me back to the ER, and would not allow them to turn me away.

A physician by the name of Dr. Aben had just came off from his vacation, walked by, touched my tummy one time. Dr. Aben, not a white male, by the way, took me into surgery, **emergency surgery, removed four feet of my small intestine. I was dying. It was gangrenous! It was green. Saved my life** right then, right there. If that had not happened and I had been sent home again, I would have died.

Nio: Sorry, so hurtful hearing that. I'm really sorry. How did you put it back together? The psychological trauma? Fact, your baby was not being cared by his mama for that little bit of time.

Adrianne: Hmm!

Nio: Knowing that you could have died.

Adrianne: I was in ICU for weeks. The psychological trauma, I can say to this day, I put that experience away. I put it so far away that I have dealt with it in parts.

Do I have a therapist? Yes, and I've had one for years. The trauma of being rejected by the hospital, rejected as a Black woman through every facet of life, remains. And so, I survive and look for ways to thrive by being excellent, and that is good, and it can be. It can be blinding in some ways as well, where you want to be so excellent that it can be maladaptive. I can take it too far. That's why you have to know thyself where it can.

You have to remember you have children to take care of. You can really take it too far, you know. Some people might drink too much. Some people might do something else too much. It just stopped all of a sudden.

Nio: Yeah. I totally understand what you're saying about taking it too far. You know, sometimes, we show up too much.

Adrianne: Yeah.

Nio: Over-processing everything. We are so calculating, every step that we over-process, you know. But how did you find? I've always known you to be joyous. So, tell me about your joy. Is there music in your joy? How do you find you? You always have that beautiful smile.

Adrianne: There is music. I am a singer/songwriter. There is the joy of raising my boys and watching their lives, watching them grow. That's where I find deep joy, and partnering and collaborating with others in my work.

CHAPTER 7

That is where I find joy that gives me value to know that the work that I've done has helped others. The underserved, the elderly, whether it's a process or an improvement in a patient, and their satisfaction, that type of situation that brings me joy.

Nio: Tell me about your singing/songwriting. What type of music? And what genre is that? Is a superpower for you? Tell me about this superpower that you have as a singer/songwriter.

Adrianne: Well, yeah, before I had to get to doing a day job. Yeah, I worked with Boys II Men back in the day, Reba McEntire, Jodie Watley, and some others. There was Rosie Perez. She was doing a movie, *The 24 Hour Woman.* So, I started to get into that world. Amazing work. James Taylor is one of my favorite singer/songwriters. Along with Elton John and Billy Joel.

Nio: This is so funny. James Taylor keeps coming up in this book as a point of joy in music. So, this is really amazing. Tell me, what did you do with those artists? And what type of music? It sounds like you did some Hip Hop. What else were you doing?

Adrianne: Oh, working with Jeremy Lubbock, Jennifer Holiday. He's an orchestra director writing music and music scores for movies in California. Used to live out there, so I used to really be 100% steeped in music, scoring, writing, woodwind instruments.

But you have to really be able to live off that. It's very expensive. And so, I began to rely more on my left brain and finishing my education. My father has. He's a registered respiratory therapist, so when he came back from Vietnam, he started his own company. And then I fell back on that healthcare administrative career.

Nio: Yeah, that is totally amazing. What's your favorite genre? What's your favorite music genre? What's your go-to when things are rough?

Adrianne: My go-to when things are rough **would be more of a James Taylor style.** It's acoustic. It's not a lot going on. It's an acoustic guitar with very good, strong lyrics; that is what I love. That's my go-to, and that brings me peace and calm. Something very different from if I'm working out. Or **I love Hip Hop,** of course. Love Hip Hop, my boys love Hip Hop; we love that. But if I need solitude and peace, and I want to reflect, great lyrics of James Taylor and **Country Music** are a good go-to for me.

Nio: I've seen you sway to Country Music. But you never told me about your music history, which is simple.

Adrianne: That's almost like a defense mechanism for me, because I've noticed some get a little weird if I divulge that part of me. People get strange. So, I said, let me not do that.

Nio: You know, you are so bright. I've been playing Classical music since I was four years old, and did my little stint in music and background singing. And I find that you have to kind of keep it to yourself, because when you start sharing, what ends up happening is there's some form of—I hate to say it—jealousy that you are multifaceted and successful at being multidimensional.

And then they basically have an attitude with you, serious attitude, that wasn't there 15 minutes before the story was shared. And it's a shame. So, as I'm sitting here, and I'm in

CHAPTER 7

my home office, and I'm looking straight at my keyboard that I keep in front 'cause that's **when I need a break from the brain, I just sit down and pound on the keyboard.** It's our quiet superpower that keeps us whole. What instrument do you still play?

Adrianne: Yes, piano, a little cello, as well.

Nio: Yeah, for me, it's piano and the harp.

Adrianne: Wow!

Nio: And you know the harp was something I actually self-taught. And then I ended up taking a few lessons. But I just fell in love with the instrument. I thought it was so beautiful. I was in church, and this woman played, and I'm like, I have to learn how to play the harp and I bought myself a Lever Harp. I started playing, looking at YouTube videos. And then I'm shocked at how I got really good at it, you know. And then I did take some lessons when I was living in Minnesota, at a wonderful school about two blocks away from the hospital. I would go and play there, and you know that's something nobody knows, right? So I know what you mean by you keep it at the vest, and it's your little secret. But here we are, both keyboardists. That's amazing.

Adrianne: That is really amazing.

Nio: Exciting. So tell me that song, that James Taylor song that you keep going back to. And, by the way, I love Reba McEntire.

Adrianne: The song I grew up on was, of course, "You've Got a Friend." Oh, James did not write that song. Carole King wrote that song. Yes, he made it famous. I remember singing that song, and there are a few others that I would need to think about that come to mind.

But "You've Got a Friend" really brought me through a lot. It's about being in solitude. What is my favorite line? I'll think about that. I'll look for that. But there is a line in the lyrics, it really helped me grow up in the meaning of what it means to be in the world and accept the good that there is in me.

Nio: It's a powerful song.

Adrianne: Because when everything is falling apart, the lyrics talk about how a true friend will be there for you, while others can be hurtful, suck away your soul, and abandon you.

Nio: Yes, that is, if we *allow* people to hurt us like that, they will.

Adrianne: That part right there?

Nio: Beautiful.

Adrianne: Yeah, I used to let them.

Nio: That is true. Triumph.

ADRIANNE'S THREE TIPS FOR SURVIVING & THRIVING WITH JOY

Adrianne shared her story, along with tips on how to overcome and live joyously, no matter what's happening in your life. Everyone has their own formula, and here is hers:

1. **Immerse in music.** As a singer/songwriter, she finds her joy in listening to music, playing it, singing it, and watching performances. Music is her private safety. You listen to what you love and find your balance in it.

2. **Focus on family.** She discovers joy in raising her boys and watching them grow and live their lives.

3. **Collaborate.** She experiences deep joy while partnering collaborating with others in her work.

How can you apply Adrianne's formula for joy in your life? And what is your superpower?

As she said, her superpower in the midst of trauma is creating, listening to, and engaging in music. The best way to bring your energy back to calmness is to use music as a channel that leads to that calm amidst chaos. So, she recommends that you **explore the power of listening in stillness. Take in the melody and words, letting the music guide your breathing as you step into the calmness of the moment.**

Her second recommendation is to **focus on family**—our most valuable life experience, because family love makes us whole. Family often comes in many forms: by blood, marriage, friendship, and support to name a few, but it is all family.

Adrianne honed into the joy of watching her boys grow and develop their passion and purpose. When life looked bleak, she was blessed with the opportunity to raise two wonderful human beings. Their lives provided perspective about what was important. This mental shift in the midst of crisis forced her to ask herself:

Are you going to move forward into what is truly valuable, or are you going to stay stuck, looking back to that moment that you can never change?

Motherhood quickly teaches you to understand that you can't control everything in life, but you can participate in the direction of growth, curiosity, inspiration, and exposure to all that is possible in life.

Adrianne's last recommendation is **Collaboration**, which means understanding that when you partner with others to meet a goal, you:

- double the talent and intellect;
- increase the energy profile; and
- intensify the joy to celebrate the accomplishment, because you are now better than you were before you started the project.

Collaboration is a win-win process because you're giving your talents, educating, and creating, while also receiving the same and learning and filling your bank. This is a two-way dialogue that will make a difference.

All of this requires the Raw Honesty that's so beautifully expressed in Country Music.

CHAPTER 8

Rock 'n Roll

Embrace Your Wild Child

Rock 'n Roll: A musical genre that originated in the 1950s, combining rhythm and blues and country, featuring high-energy lyrics about love, politics, and society with heavy, repetitive beats and instruments including guitar, bass, and drums.

A woman who embodies the lively, exuberant energy of Rock 'n Roll is **Jenny Davies**. She is a fearless spirit and is not shy to look in the mirror. Jenny lives in Joy. She does not need the acceptance from the group at large. She always has an honest smile because she lives from her authentic self.

Jenny started her career in accounting with her Associate's Degree from Mcintosh College. She later graduated from Boston College with a Bachelor of Science in biology and returned to school to follow her passion and purpose at the Institute for Professional Excellence in Coaching and received her Professional Coaching Certification and ELI-MP Certification.

JOY NOTES

Jenny and I met at a Healthcare Financial Management Association event for the Massachusetts-Rhode Island Chapter (HFMA MA-RI). I was attending my first event after moving to the area, and there she was, a beam of light with her signature smile.

"Welcome," she said like she meant it. I knew no one, but she took my arm and introduced me to board members and any one she could. It was a spinning-top moment, but oh, so fun.

That's when I knew that the word that defined her was FUN. We shared life and business history and connected. At the time, I was on my purpose journey after the two cardiac arrests, I discovered the **Institute for Professional Excellence in Coaching (iPEC)** and embarked on the education path to becoming a certified coach. I shared the information with Jenny, and of course, she happened to be doing research on coaching at the time and we shared that purpose and all the fulfilling enlightenment that it provided.

She is a natural giver and an excellent listener, which makes her a great coach. Her story is powerful, because it explains how to use grace, fun, and joy to transcend. Her recommendations are inspiring and easily available to us all. Enjoy her interview:

Niobis Queiro: Jenny Davies is going to tell us about her joy and her survival of trauma. So, Jenny, thank you so much for your time, and joining me in this conversation. Can you please tell me your story about how you came through cancer, and still derived the highest number of joyous smiles in your life.

Jenny Davies: Sure, I'm happy to share that story with you, Nio. So, I know one of the questions that you had asked was around, "What was the trauma, and what was the triumph?"

Nio: Yes, do share.

Jenny: Okay, so the trauma for me was that, honestly, before I knew anything about a cancer diagnosis, I would have told you that I was in the best shape of my life. I really would have. I had lots of energy; I was exercising regularly. I was going to Tai Chi a couple times a week with my husband. So, I was in great shape. I wouldn't have known that there was a thing wrong with me, and unexpectedly got a finding. Well, I guess it started out as a finding on a mammogram that had nothing to do with the ovarian cancer. But it was something that happened that coincided. And I think God made these things happen for a reason.

So, the year before, I had missed my annual exam because one of my family members was going through some healthcare issues. And so, I was focused on my family member and not on myself, which I think is such a common thing with women, that **we kind of ignore ourselves, because we're caring.**

That's that level of energy, right? We're caring for somebody else, so **we're not focused on our own well-being. And so I missed my own annual exam.** The year was coming to a close, so in December, I had my mammogram. And the mammogram showed an abnormality that they wanted to follow up with the diagnostic mammograms, and this had happened to me about 10 years before. I was not super excited about going back for the diagnostic mammograms and whatever was next.

So, I was kind of putting it off. And when the radiology department called again to ask about scheduling a follow-up, I said, "You know what? I want to make an appointment with my regular primary care before I come back for more tests."

And so I did make an appointment with my primary care practitioner, who was a nurse practitioner, who I had seen for a very long time. I made the appointment for her, which was at the end of February, and when I went in to see her, I was telling her all that was going on, and she was really reassuring.

"You know, you really have to go back for these diagnostic mammograms," she said, "and whatever comes next, it's in your best interest to do that."

So, while I was there, of course she did the internal exam, and she said:

"You know, Jenny, I want you to follow up with an abdominal ultrasound, because I'm feeling something pressing down on your cervix."

"I wouldn't have suspected that there was a thing wrong with me," I said. So I wasn't at all worried about what she was telling me. I'd had fibroids before, so I just figured it was another fibroid, and kind of dismissed it from being anything.

"Is it okay if I follow up with this like in a month after I have the diagnostic mammograms and whatever is happening with that?" I asked.

"Absolutely, that's fine," she said.

And so that's what I did. Before I left the office that day, I very intentionally made the appointment for a month later, on the same day that I was taking my mom, who was close to 90 years old at the time, to some appointments.

So, a month later I go to the same office, the office where it was my GYN practice for the ultrasound, and I hadn't met the ultrasound tech before. It was the first time meeting her, and I'm kind of chatty; I get it. And I was talking with her when she was doing the ultrasound, and I could see she was outlining what I thought was my abdomen. I don't know what she's doing, so I was just asking her questions. She wasn't very forthcoming, but I just thought because I didn't know, or I just thought she's just not very forthcoming with information. I didn't really think anything of it. So, then she was all done.

CHAPTER 8

I went in to get dressed, and when I came out there was another person in the room. I didn't know she was a doctor at the time, so I just thought they were getting ready for their next patient. I said my goodbyes and started to leave. The second woman who was in the office introduced herself as my doctor, who I also had not met before.

"Can you please sit down?" she asked.

So I sat down on the exam table. She pulled her chair up close to me and she started sharing the news that they had found a large mass, like she was emphasizing the word large, and she was holding her hands like this. And, you know, I could kind of feel myself floating up out of my body and watching, like you get Disconnected from yourself. I could feel myself watching it from above. And I knew that I wasn't really connecting at all with her. I paused and I asked her, "Can you please write things down for me?"

Because I wasn't processing information very well, and even just going back and recalling this, it's definitely causing me some distress. You can probably see it. And so she wrote down on little pieces of paper what she had been telling me.

She was going to send me for some blood tests before I left the office, and they were also going to be referring me to a GYN/Oncologist, and I'm not sure that I had ever even heard of that specialty before. So, I got the blood test before I left, and then I had to take my mom to her appointments, and I couldn't tell my mom anything, because I didn't really know anything yet, and I didn't want to worry her. Before the end of the day, I got the test results from those lab tests, and the doctor had actually left a voicemail message for me, telling me that one of the tests showed an elevated level.

In that moment, I was thinking, *How much life insurance do I have? And how many years left to pay off my mortgage?* Those two thing popped into my mind. And I was thinking about my husband, like, *Am I going to leave him as a widower?*

I had never heard of anybody who had survived ovarian cancer before. The only people that I ever heard of that had ovarian cancer were Gilda Radner and Madeline Kahn, and of course, they both died of it. I went to an art class that evening. You know, you wanna just keep doing your regular stuff. And then I went home, and I can kind of still picture my hand on the doorknob as I went into my house. I knew that as soon as I shared the information with my husband, that our lives would never be the same again, and they haven't. But in some ways, in a really good way, it's just changed life a lot, so he was really comforting. You know he was.

I was bawling when I was telling him what was going on, and he said, "You know what? We don't know anything yet."

And I said, "Well, we know one thing. I know that they're not gonna leave that big mass inside my abdomen. We know that."

And he said, "Okay, we know that."

So within a week, we had an appointment with a GYN/Oncologist here at Bay State. And I was honestly, totally unprepared for what I was about to hear. So, I went in, and there's a lot to the story. But ultimately, she sat us down in her office. She did an internal exam as well, and she had the lab tests, and she probably had more information than I even will ever know about. She sat on one side of her desk. We were sitting on the other side, and there was also a nurse and a medical fellow in the room. To me, [the desk] seemed like a big chasm between us.

She had in front of her, so that I could see it, a diagram of a woman's reproductive system, and she was going through all the possibilities, like it could be Stage 1 cancer, you know. All the different stages of cancer that it could be, and she was drawing so that I could understand what was going to happen.

One of the things, probably the worst of it for me, was that this large mass was laying on a portion of my bowel and there was a very real possibility that I was going to need an ostomy. And that scared me actually more than the idea of cancer. I don't know why, but it just scared me even more than the idea of cancer, and the news was so overwhelming to me.

I think I said out loud: "I've taken such good care of myself my whole life, and now you're going to ruin my body."

That's how I was interpreting it, and I started bawling, like, I did the ugly cry that you never wanna have anybody see. And the doctor and the nurse and the medical fellow all got up and they left the room, so it was only my husband and me, and he stayed to comfort me. But it was such a lonely feeling. They just got up and left me, got up and left the room. I think they wanted to give me my privacy while I had this ugly cry. But I was like crumpled, honestly, as crumpled as the word that comes to mind for me.

So, he stayed and comforted me, and then eventually the nurse, who looked like an angel, came back in the room, and she said, "Look, we really know what we're doing here."

And what I realized afterward is that what they really wanted from me was to sign the informed consent. I was up against a lot, and they wanted me to sign the informed consent so that they weren't going to delay anything. And so, I totally got it by the time that I was leaving like, oh, they want to be assigned the informed consent, because they want to move this process along.

So I signed the informed consent, and I had to go for some more lab tests. I had to go for a chest X-ray, and they wanted me to get a CT scan. So, before I even left the building, one of their coordinators helped me to line up all of this stuff. I said to my husband, "I'm not going to be the one to delay this. I'm not going to draw this out. I get this is really serious." So, within a couple of days, I had these tests lined up.

I'm pretty sure I went back to work after that doctor's visit. I'm pretty certain that I did, and I had to share this news with the person that I reported to at the time. She no longer works here, but I had to share it with her, because I was going to need eight weeks of recovery. I would never have thought I would need eight weeks for anything. But she told me I was going to need an eight-week recovery window. And then, after the eight weeks, if I needed chemotherapy, which was not a given, they would start the chemotherapy like six to eight weeks after, maybe five to eight weeks after my surgery. That was on a Thursday. The following Friday, I had my surgery. They told me it could be three weeks out, depending on how they would schedule the ORs. It was one week. That's what it was for me, so I think that my case was probably pretty urgent, because I don't think that they would have rushed me in there if it hadn't been.

So I had my surgery, and I came through it really well, and mercifully, I did not need that ostomy. When I woke up from the surgery, my husband and my sister, my younger sister, were there in the recovery room, pre-pandemic, in 2015. I don't even know if they let people in recovery rooms anymore.

Anyway, at the time, it was, and so they were there, and they were the ones who shared with me that it was cancer. My doctor wasn't there, because she must have had other surgeries, but my husband and my sister were there, and they were both crying. In that moment, Nio, I think I had a level seven moment. Then, I had a moment that it was like, I was completely at peace. I was not crying. The fact that it was cancer, it didn't land heavy on me. I just thought, *Okay, this is what it is*. At least I didn't have to have the ostomy. So maybe a little level seven, little level three. A little mix there, reflecting on myself from the past.

So that was the trauma. And then, once I was past that surgery, I healed really well. I was in great shape beforehand, so I healed really well. I spent a few days in the hospital and went home. I did need chemotherapy, so they staged it. We

CHAPTER 8

went for a second opinion. My husband and me, out to Dana Farber [Cancer Institute in Boston], and I'm going to back up two giant steps again.

So, before I knew anything about a cancer diagnosis at all, I had been planning on going to a reunion of a comedy and improv group that I had performed with in college. I didn't know anything about anything at that time. That was probably late in 2014. So, somebody was getting this group together. And it's like, "Oh, yes, I'll be there, definitely. I'm really looking forward to it." And I was, so when I knew I had to have surgery, I can kind of remember being in the building where I work, talking to my nurse and asking her before my surgery, "Am I going to be able to go to this reunion now?" I wanted to know whether or not she thought I was gonna be able to pull it off or not.

To her credit, she said, "Jenny, I think you should plan to go and be with your friends and have fun."

So, I kind of had that in my mind that that's what I was going to do.

My surgery was on April 10th, and I think the reunion was on April 28th, and I was able to go. I was well enough to go to Boston. I live in Western Mass. We went to Boston for the reunion. I was still healing, but I felt well enough to be there, and it was so much fun watching improv and playing improv games, like it was just so much fun. And I remember in the moment, and again, I think maybe level seven, right? I was watching myself, having this moment and knowing this is what I want. I want more of that. **I want more laughter. I want more joy. I want to be having fun.**

You have to give yourself permission to laugh and have fun in the midst of trauma. I don't want to be thinking about this diagnosis. I don't want to be dwelling on this diagnosis, and I definitely don't want to be talking to other people who have the same diagnosis. **I want to just be laughing**

and having fun, and so on. On our way home, I was already scheming about, "How do I join an improv group?" And I didn't really know how that was going to happen. But somehow, miraculously, it did so.

I had to find a creative outlet. I had to take a step to do me, to take care of me.

There was a cancer outreach in our community called Cancer Connections. We don't have it anymore, but at the time, they had **an improv group that met in a community room** once a week on a Thursday. I signed up for it, and I'm certain that I was the only one in active treatment who was in this group, and it was like so much fun, like it was such joy meeting with this group of women and just going and having fun and laughing, and it was an appointment on my schedule every single week.

So that was my default, right? I was gonna go there every single week. My chemotherapy appointments were on Wednesdays and started at the end of May, and I got to meet with these women. Chemotherapy on Wednesday, bounced right back, went to work on Thursday, and then went to improv after work every Thursday. A lot like the human spirit, just so amazing and beautiful, we can get used to anything. I really think we can get used to almost anything.

Before long, that started to feel like a routine to me. I go to chemo, and then I go to improv. And it was just like, okay, I go do this, and then I go have fun. And it was. It was, really. It added something to my life that I probably wouldn't have done if this diagnosis hadn't happened to me.

And I will tell you, honestly, that it was something that was on my bucket list that I was like, I'm not really brave enough to do this, but when my life was almost taken from me, I leaned into it. I found somewhere in this vulnerability. For me, there was a gift, and this was at least part of the gift. The other part of the gift, quite honestly, is we work in a very conservative profession, right? And I would say of myself, this probably is not true of everybody, but I would say of myself, *If there's some sparkle in my personality that I was not comfortable having the people around me necessarily be privy to, that was something that I kind of kept to myself.*

And especially in another department that I had worked in, in the organization that I work for, I kind of stuffed that down. And I didn't let everybody see that. But after my diagnosis with ovarian cancer, it became so clear to me that if I didn't show people how much I love them, and who I really am, I may never have a chance to do that. So I stopped stuffing down that authenticity, and I let this sparkle shine, and I think becoming a professional coach is like another iteration of that for me, like, how much can this beacon shine, right? If I don't let this beacon shine, then the whole world is gonna miss it. I think I'm just being called to do something more at this point in my life.

Nio: What would you tell a woman who was going through some trauma? It doesn't have to necessarily be cancer, but some trauma.

Jenny: Somebody asked me a question. I was at the Women's Conference, the HFMA, a year ago, maybe not quite a year ago. She had asked the panelists, "Who are the speakers about?" Kind of how to present themselves in their office, in their work environment.

And I can't really remember the response that the panel gave, but it was a convoluted response. I remember turning to her at a break time, and I said, "I really appreciated the question that you asked, and I'm gonna tell you my answer to your question. Live without regret, or try to live with less regret."

So, I think I would say the same thing to other women who are going through something traumatic, or just going through a transition, or just trying to think about how they're living. Try to live with less regret, because it's the things that you don't do, that you wish you did. You may not have another chance. Or, not showing somebody how it is that you show up with energy at a thousand watts. Right? Who else does that, right?

So, try to live with less regret. I tell people more often how much I care about them, and I show them by the way that I show up. I don't know how to be less than myself. I think that in the past, I have been less than myself, because I've stuffed down some of that authenticity, some of that beautiful sparkle that you see.

Nio: That was a great story.

Jenny: The other story that I had shared with you, I think was the story about the day that I got my hair cut off. I'll send you a picture of myself. I used to wear my hair in a bob, and, I am telling you, people would stop me all the time and ask me about my beautiful hair. And it was really beautiful. I would have told you at the time that my hair was my best feature, without a question, without a shadow of a doubt. My hair was definitely my best feature. And I knew it was going to fall out because, they don't tell you this, but your scalp starts to hurt. Mine did, anyway. The breeze would blow, and my hair would really hurt. So, if I was walking in the park, I would have to wear a little ball cap. My hair actually started falling out on a Sunday. My scalp had been hurting for a couple of days. I got into the shower on a Sunday, and it started coming out in handfuls. And I could kind of feel myself getting weak in the knees, seeing these handfuls of hair coming out. It was pretty tough to take, so I got out of the shower and wrapped myself up in a towel. I was shaking like a leaf, and sat down on the bed and I told my husband. He, honestly, was so comforting.

CHAPTER 8

He came and sat down next to me, and I still had a lot of hair on my head, and he was like, "What are you talking about? You still have a lot of hair."

And I said, "Go, look."

He did. He was like, "Oh, yeah, that is a lot that fell out." So he understood.

And I said, "I don't really know what to do, because my hairdresser doesn't work on Sunday, and she doesn't work on Monday," and my plan was to go and have her take care of this. Buzz my hair off.

So he said, "Why don't you wait for your sister to come?"

I said okay. I think he was, in retrospect, having an intuition that my sister would be able to come up with a plan. I'm going to show you a picture of my sister. This is my sister, Helen, and then her partner, June, is there. My sister Helen and I are almost Irish twins. We're born a year and a week apart, so our birthdays are right next to each other on the calendar. Just to tell you a little bit more: On Monday, we had gone back to Tai Chi. I was going through chemotherapy and my doctor had cleared me to go back to work, and she cleared me to go back to Tai Chi. So, the Sunday that my hair started falling out, the very next day, I was going back to work. I hadn't been to work in eight weeks, and I'm going back to work the very next day, and my hair is falling out in handfuls. So, Monday, after work, I tried calling my hairdresser again, and Monday evening, we went to Tai Chi, 'cause that was what we did before my surgery. While I was at Tai Chi without my phone, my hairdresser called. So I missed my opportunity to connect with her. I was like, all right, I'm just gonna wait until my sister comes and see what we can do.

So I went to chemo with my sister, Helen, who actually lives in Maine, by the way. She came all the way to Western Massachusetts, because she wanted to take me to one of my appointments.

I said, "Sure, come in, come and take me to one of my appointments."

By now, this would be like my fourth treatment, I think. Maybe my sixth treatment, something like that. By this time, I've been wearing a Wonder Woman t-shirt to my chemo appointments very intentionally. You gotta get something that's lower than your port, which was right there, something that's comfortable. So, I got a Wonder Woman t-shirt. Helen and I went to chemo, the infusion suite, and we were telling my nurse, Mary, what was going on. Mary was really reassuring in a way that made me laugh, like she kind of got me. And she said, "You know, Jenny, you would get more than one haircut if you wanted to, because you're not keeping it, anyway." She did make us laugh.

And my sister, Helen, said, "Jenny, you could get a mohawk if you wanted to, with lightning bolts buzzed in the side."

Then it was like a challenge. And I said, "You know what, Helen, I could get a mohawk if I wanted. Why not?" I did have my wig in my bag, because we were gonna go to the hairdresser at some point that day and get my hair cut off. So my sister, my brilliant sister, called around and tried to figure out, because she doesn't live locally, where could I go and get my hair cut? And one of her friends who still lives in the area, made a recommendation. So, after my chemo appointment, the two of us go to a hair salon in a mall that's very close to the area, and I walked up to the reception desk and told the receptionist what I wanted, and she kind of bristled a little bit. She was taken aback, and I said:

"Well, this is what's happening. I'm going through chemotherapy, so I'm losing my hair anyway, and just thought it would be kind of fun to do this."

You know, have something to kind of smile about. I told her that I had a wig in my bag and I would put my wig on. The manager of the salon, her name was Anna, walked over to me

CHAPTER 8

and she said, "We're gonna give you a great haircut and you're gonna wanna leave here with the haircut that we give you."

So I just kind of shrugged my shoulders. I was in disbelief. I sat down. She put the cape on me and she buzzed my hair off into a modified mohawk, and I had the biggest smile on my face, because my scalp wasn't hurting. The weight of all that hair was off, and that's kind of a metaphor, right? **Like the weight of something that you're holding onto is holding you down.** It's such a nice metaphor. It's very powerful.

Nio: You shed the old person.

Jenny: You can see, I've never let that hair grow back. I still have that vibe. Then, a younger hairdresser, Vivian, walked over to me and she said, "Ordinarily, Jenny, there's a barber here and he would buzz a symbol in the side of your hair. He's not here today, do you want to come back another day?"

And I said, "Oh, I really can't, Vivian. I just went back to work on Monday. This is my day off to get my chemo, and I don't even know if I'm gonna have hair next week. So this is my day."

So she said, "Well, I've never done this before, but if you're willing to trust me, I'll give it a try."

And I started laughing, and I said, "You know what, Vivian, if you mess it up on this side, you can just buzz it off. We'll try it again on the other side."

So, the two of us were laughing, and I said, "I'm wearing my Wonder Woman shirt." I just kind of pointed out the symbol on my shirt, and she said, "I don't even need it."

Nio: I carry the Wonder Woman symbol on my keychain, and I draw comic book art as my hobby.

Jenny: In that moment, I realized that God had really put me in the hands of these people who were going to help me. I don't even know how. How is that even possible that I landed in the hands of these people who were taking such good care of me? So, she buzzed a modified "W" into the side of my hair. It looked awesome, and I absolutely walked out of there with that haircut, and didn't even think about putting the wig on.

Occasionally, I would wear [my natural hair] to work, but mostly I would wear my wig to work. The reason was that, because I work in a healthcare organization, I didn't want people to be thinking of me as a patient. I wanted them to be thinking of me as their colleague, and so I would pencil in my eyebrows, which had also fallen out, and I would put on a wig, just so they wouldn't get nervous about me.

This is another thing about me. I never thought of myself as sick. I just said, *I'm fighting cancer.* So, I don't like the word "sick." That was not for me. I just was fighting cancer.

The doctor that I saw for the second opinion, she got my personality in a way that I think my own doctor didn't quite understand. I was nervous about asking my own doctor about my prognosis, because she was the one that got up and left the room when I started crying. But I was more comfortable with the doctor for my second opinion, and I said:

"I've read that when ovarian cancer is caught in the early stages, there's a 90% cure rate."

And she said, "Well, that is true. But you're not in the early stage. You're in the 50-50 club."

My immediate reaction, without even thinking about it, was, "I'm in the good 50. I'm not even thinking about that other 50."

And she said, "You know what? That's a really healthy way for you to be thinking. And that's the way I want you to continue to think."

She said, "If there's something more that's going to be needed, we're the experts, and we'll figure it out. You just worry about what you're doing right now."

CHAPTER 8

And so, I kind of had that in my mind, too.

That evening, after I got my hair cut off, my husband, my mother, my sister, and my sister's friend—who had connected us with the hair salon—and I went out to a very crowded restaurant, and I did not have my wig on. I had this Wonder Woman hairdo and we had dinner together, and we were belly-laughing at the table and sharing stories. My sister, Helen, and her buddy, Linda, were making all of us laugh.

These experiences taught me that **whatever is going on in your life, you could be experiencing joy.** That joy is there just for you to experience. You don't have to turn your back on joy. It's there. You just have to maybe seek it out and recognize that it's still there for you. So, we had a lovely dinner together.

At the very end of the night, my husband and I, on our way home, stopped at the CVS pharmacy because the Benadryl would help with some of that sleeplessness that I would experience when I had chemotherapy. So I popped into the CVS by myself and I almost ran smack into a woman who was coming down the aisle in the opposite direction. She was like somebody that I would describe as a soccer mom. She was adorable, cute, blonde, with a little white skirt, and she had a reaction when she saw me, like she was taken aback. So I was a little self-conscious about what I must look like, and I was very curious at that point what I looked like. When I got the Benadryl and we went home, my first stop was to go to the bathroom mirror, because I wanted to see what I looked like. And, Nio, it was like I was seeing myself for the very first time in some ways. I had this moment of self-recognition, like I had never seen myself before, and my reaction when I saw myself was, *I look like a rock star without hair. How about that?*

Before, I would have told you that my hair was my best feature, and then, after that, it was like, oh, my hair was not my best feature, not by a long shot. My sense of humor, my personal strength, my smile—those are my best features. Yeah, so it made me really recognize myself.

Through that vulnerability, I had this self-recognition that I'm not sure that I ever would have had, [if] this diagnosis not been placed in my path. I maybe would have ignored it for a very long time. And there are some other transitions that I'm sharing with you that are maybe on the horizon for me.

I feel like God is putting this in my path because He wants more of me. He wants me to be a more authentic version of myself. And I would have to venture to say, maybe a better version of myself. I don't know if it's better, or if there's a more aware version of yourself in there. You know what I mean. It's already in there. It's just, we live in such a conservative [environment] in healthcare finance. We are in the most conservative of the conservatives, and it is a struggle to be authentic. When we first met, I gravitated towards you because I had that energy. It was that level six energy that carried. And I said, "Oh, there's somebody that's comfortable in her skin."

I didn't see that in the others. They were all kind of copycats of each other, and comfortable. The word was comfortable, which means you don't vary from the norm. You make others feel comfortable with you, and you're comfortable, because you're not rocking the boat. And there's nothing wrong with that. It's what finance is. It's dollars and cents, and making sure that you don't make a variation. But, God, there's so much more to life. And there's not so much more to do.

Nio: One more question for you. Through this, was there any song that made you giggle, that made you feel alive?

Jenny: Yes. So, when I was in the hospital, there was a patient care technician, and I wish I could remember her name. I'll have to look on the roster and see if I can find her name. Or maybe it's in my journal that I kept at the time. She would

CHAPTER 8

play a song for me to lift my spirits, and it's a song that, now, every time I hear it, it lifts my spirits, because I realize how far I've come. It was Bruno Mars "Uptown Funk."

More recently, within the last two years, I started going to Aqua Zumba at my gym. I am very physically fit, and I work at it. I'm very intentional about staying physically fit. Aqua Zumba is physical fitness and a party at the same time, 'cause they play fun music and you get to dance for an hour in the water, so it feels effortless.

And, this is another metaphor for life . . . that when you're exercising in water, you're actually working harder than if you were working just in the air. But, at least for me, there's a feeling of effortlessness that's there, because it's so much fun to be dancing in the water for an hour, and nobody can see what you're doing, because you're underwater. So it's really delightful.

And the song that just makes me laugh every time I hear it is by Fergie; it's called "A Little Party Never Killed Nobody." In the song, she's telling a man to decide if he wants to be with her in that moment, because the present moment is all we have, so enjoy it by dancing and partying right now.

[I might sing it] off key, but I don't even care. It doesn't matter. It's that song that frees you. And all of a sudden you can feel. And immediately you were like, *Yeah, okay, this is good.* Fergie's letting you feel. And that's what music does. It brings us back to our core nature.

Yeah, there's a James Taylor song that I would listen to. Well, I like James Taylor, and there was one, and it was one that made me feel, in a different way, like it didn't make me feel like I wanted to dance and sing. It just made me feel like a reflection in the moment. The song is, "Secret of Life." It's about learning to enjoy life's journey.

I haven't listened to it in a long time, but it makes me pause and reflect, and I do. I am so intentional at this point in my life about scheduling things that I think are going to be fun, **saying yes to more things that I think will be fun.** Or maybe, you're going to scare me, but make me feel like I'm going to be bigger than I am right now. I think there's more for me. And I think that's why I didn't get that. I think that's why I didn't die of my cancer diagnosis, Nio, because God wasn't done with me.

Nio: And I agree with you. I know for a fact that when we are going through these extreme situations, God has more for us to do. Life is a joy passage. And the purpose of life is to open up your heart.

Jenny: Yeah, yeah. And I actually remember, how I told you at the beginning, my nurse practitioner found the mass, but then it was through an ultrasound that it was confirmed. I just saw her on Thursday night when I was doing storytelling. She happened to be there in the audience. I didn't know that. She happened to be there in the audience, and I was sharing with her.

It's been eight years since I finished my chemotherapy and stories are so powerful, Nio. So, her partner, Nina, and I attended a storytelling class together, and Nina shared with me, she said, "Well, I think you might know my partner." So she was telling me a little bit about her partner, and I said:

"I actually think I do know her. I think she saved my life."

And that experience taught me, tell your story, because you never know how your story is going to land for another person. And by me telling her that story, it opened up something else for her.

Nio: Amazing. Thank you for sharing your story. It is the beginning of that opening for you to tell all your stories, and really write that book, because you have so much to share. And it's so powerful.

CHAPTER 8

Jenny: Thank you. I would say, honestly, one of the things that I learned is by leaning into my vulnerability, I found my power. I mean, that's one thing that I really learned. And the other is that joy is present, regardless of what else is happening. Somehow, most people want to focus on what's wrong and what they don't want, and it's so much more powerful when we can lean into what it is that we do want, and find it and make time for it.

Nio: I think you are extremely wise, and it's one of the detriments that we do in healthcare. We always talk about all the things that are wrong. We forget to celebrate that which is good and what we've learned from the situations. And since I'm part of our modern healthcare system, I think about the beginnings of healthcare, and it focused on people being charitable toward one another. That's the only reason that it existed.

There were people who were professional beggars, basically trying to figure out, okay, how do we get the money to open a hospital, because people need these services? And the more modern we've become, the more complicated we've made things. But really, maybe we just need to become professional beggars again. I say it all the time.

Jenny: We need to get back to our mission and vision.

Nio: And getting from the heart and not from judgment. There was a time, I remember when my mother was diagnosed with cancer. And I remember her doctor hugging her. You would never see that today, unfortunately; I'm talking about when you're giving the news, it's rare that you would see that type of connection today. That's all I'm trying to say. Yes, of course there's some doctors that have it. And it's understandable. I mean, how much of themselves can they put out there?

They'd be totally stripped of their energy by giving it away like that. But what I'm trying to say is, there is a balance that we can reach, especially if we're present. And you gave some beautiful nuggets about vulnerability and being present, and through it all, owning your joy.

JENNY'S THREE TIPS FOR SURVIVING & THRIVING WITH JOY

Jenny shared her story, along with tips on how to overcome and live joyously, no matter what's happening in your life. Everyone has their own formula, and here is hers:

1. **Get or stay physically fit**. She does aqua Zumba at my gym.

2. **Set the intention and say yes to things that are fun**.

3. **Have a sense of humor**; make sure you laugh often and hard.

How can you apply Jenny's recipe for joy in your life?

Her first action step to **"Get or stay physically fit"** seems simple, but it is very difficult. Why? Because we excuse our way out of this commitment that requires intention, perseverance, time, energy and dedication to yourself. Plus you have to find what exercise and eating methodology is the best fit for you and your lifestyle.

Fitness is a dedicated self-investment that impacts your mind, body, and spirit. Physical fitness was the saving force in her personal health journey. If you are fit, you have a better chance to overcome when your body gets weary. You can persevere against emotions that can otherwise overrun you. Fitness energizes your spirit. You know how to get the high from a good workout. You know how to handle pain, as it is temporary, and exercise helps you push through to the other side where you can triumph over the trauma.

Jenny's second tip is one to sit with for a moment. She says to **"Set the INTENTION to say YES for things that are FUN."**

How many times have we stopped ourselves from going to an event because we prefer to stay home and nurse our misery? There is so much more power to open the door to fun when you are at your lowest. We tell ourselves lies such as, *I'll be a buzz kill.* The best option is to attend, be present in the moment, and join in on the fun.

The secret is that it is up to you. The more that you engage in fun, the more that you can experience joy, because you find ways to define it for yourself. If you do not expose yourself to positive experiences, you only know negativity. I know that's obvious, but when you are lost or in the dumps, you need all the tools you can get, because today this approach is the right approach for the situation and tomorrow another approach is just right to arm yourself with the freedom of options.

Jenny's last words of wisdom are, **"Laugh till it hurts."** Laughter can cure heartache. So many studies prove with neuroscience evidence that laughter is therapeutic. For example, The NeuroscienceNews.com published a paper in June 2023 called, "Laughter as Medicine: Humor Therapy Reduces Depression and Anxiety Symptoms," by Sara Henning-Stout. The project was comprised of 29 individual studies from nine countries involving almost 3,000 participants who had depression, anxiety, or both. The study included groups of children undergoing surgery, people with chronic conditions, and older participants in nursing homes. The study concluded that humor therapy provided significant reduction in the individuals' depression and anxiety.

But most of us do not need a study to tell us what we have experienced on our own. I remember sitting in the funeral home at my dad's wake and out of nowhere my grandson came up to me and said:

"Knock, knock."

"Who's there?" I asked.

"I am," he said.

"I am who?" I asked.

"I am who's knocking!" he said.

"Who are you?" I asked, roaring in laughter. (PS: we also got in trouble with my mom. She gave us the look. We quickly walked out of the room.)

It was so unexpected and clever for a four-year-old. That moment freed me from the sorrow of the situation that I had no idea how to handle. I remember kissing and hugging my grandson, overwhelmed with pure gratitude. How did he know I needed a joke? He was my hero!

So remember, one of the best ways to hit a *Joy Note*, is to laugh freely, often, and hard.

CHAPTER 9

Shit Creek Survivor

Top 40: the current 40 most popular songs in a particular genre.

Top 40 music is a celebration of all music genres, and reflects the most popular songs that Americans are enjoying on any given day. This list is especially helpful for folks who usually listen to one genre, because Top 40 hits include many musical genres, such as The Blues, Disco, and Rock.

My dear friend **Deb Stall**, like many of us, personifies qualities of many types of music, all combining to create the symphony that is her personality and life story.

Deb is one of the most unique artistic women I know. There is nothing Deb can't do! She's an expert in Revenue Cycle Service, and if she is part of the team, you will succeed, whether her role is the COO, SVP of Sales, or consultant. You would think that is enough, but her skills reach far beyond the boardroom and business affairs.

Deb owns an alpaca farm—Dixon Creek Farm—whose store offers incredible yarn and knit designs from alpaca

JOY NOTES

wool, as well as looms and other knitting equipment. Deb also creates scented candles, along with organic soaps and lotions. And she's an accomplished chef. I can't do her justice. Deb represents the Top 40, because she's present, innovative, enlightening, and joyous.

Deb and I met more than 15 years ago on the consulting front. She recruited me to join her on a stressful project. We made magic happen and created a lifelong friendship. Deb does not settle for "good enough." She is always growing, developing, and overcoming all drama. I've learned fortitude and tenacity from her. I was so blessed by her willingness to share a season of her life with us.

Deb Stall: Let's do this thing.

Nio: I'm here with my lovely friend Deb Stall, and we are going to go through her journey of rising from trauma—ridiculous trauma—into triumph. Just a remark.

Deb: Great way to put it, Nio. You want to hear about the cancer journey, right? March 28th, I went to check on a place that I thought, frankly, was a hemorrhoid for months and months, and they immediately sent me to a surgeon the next day to have it removed and biopsied, because they said it's absolutely not a hemorrhoid.

The waiting time when going through that is so hard, and I had to wait two weeks for the tissue biopsy to come back, and it came back as cancerous—the rare form of rectal cancer. We didn't know how extensive it was, so I went immediately to have a CT scan done, and that's when they saw that it was already in the lymph nodes and other parts of my body.

They actually diagnosed me at Stage 4. I think some doctors will probably say Stage 3, but my oncologist and surgeon said Stage 4. That was hard news to take and, naive as I was, I

CHAPTER 9

did not know that the treatment was going to be even worse than anything I've ever been through in my life. They prescribed six weeks of radiation—which was Monday through Friday, five days a week, for six weeks—and then chemo two different times, and I got it through a port.

It was really hard. I got second degree burns from the cancer, actually. The radiation burned me really bad and, according to my oncologist, having cancer in those areas, and even in your esophagus, are the two worst places that you can ever have cancer, from a pain-level perspective.

Nio: You were just in a new job while you were going through this.

Deb: Right. The thing is, well, I was doing contract work and things like that, but I worked all through it. I didn't skip a beat, and it was hard for me to sometimes focus on getting out of bed every day. Your focus becomes different when you're going through something like that and normal life, you're like, *Okay, what do I have to do tomorrow?*

Plan your day, blah, blah, but going through that, it's like, how do I just get through the day without so much pain? How can I sit in one place for more than five minutes and be comfortable? How do I get from an hour-and-a-half drive one way to radiation every day without just crying in pain? I avoided pain medication because it makes me sick. I truly had a hard time with managing the pain, but I got through it.

I think one of the things that was the most upsetting to me was that I had a partner in life that I thought would be there with me, had committed to sticking around and helping me through the cancer, managing the farm. By the way, I have a 30-acre alpaca farm [Dixon Creek Farm] that requires daily maintenance. Well, my partner left the week before I started treatment, so that was truly hard for me to understand. I had a level of understanding that I just couldn't get to, and you just don't understand what people think or what they go through or why they would leave a spouse or a partner, and even his 18-year-old son, for that matter, without even saying goodbye.

That was hard, but you know what? I did it. I got through it and with the help of people like you, Nio, and **friends and family** who truly stepped up, checked on me, sent me food, cooked for me, and sent care packages. I mean, I still order from that place that [my friend sent me food from]. It's just a wonderful, warm thing to do for somebody, but those are the things that I remember, instead of the pain. It's just like having a baby. You go through all that pain of having a child. You're like, *Oh, my God, I'll never do this again!*

And people do it over and over again, so you forget the pain, but what you do remember is what people did for you during that time. The friends that step up, the people that text you, call you, email you, write to you, people I haven't heard from—and I can't tell you how long—and just the care that I felt during that time was overwhelming.

I think, truly, Nio, **that's what got me through all that.** It really, truly was. Yeah, the work was a little distracting for me, too, but it truly was the friends and family that stepped up. My sister and my niece came, they alternated weeks. My best friend, Teresa, came, you came, Beth came, my cousin Lisa came, my three sons took alternate weeks to take me back and forth. Taking care of the farm is just an undertaking. Meanwhile, I'm laid up in the bed feeling like I'm worthless and don't know if I want to live or die, and the things that go through your mind, it changes your perspective on everything.

Nio: What would you tell a woman who learns news like this? What would be your message to her?

CHAPTER 9

Deb: **Stay positive**. Stay positive is one message, and the next message would be, **do not give up**.

Do not let those nighttime thoughts creep into your mind and take over. That happened to me at the beginning, especially during the abandonment time. I got angry, I got mad, and that helped, too. Sometimes that just jolts you back into reality to say, *You know what? You're going to do this, you're going to show your family that you can do this, show your friends you can get through this, and look forward to the other side of it, because it truly is a blessing from God*. It also changes the way you think about faith. This is more testimonial than anything, but I have not been as good of a Christian as I should have been. I grew up in the Baptist church in Louisiana, so every time the doors were open, I was there as a child. My grandfather was a Baptist minister, but as an adult, you kind of get away from that, but here on the farm, an alpaca farm, you worship in a different way, and I became closer to God. I pray, I pray for others, that's also something that helps. I would tell someone if they're going through this, just don't forget your faith and keep on trucking.

I mean, I just can't tell you how important it is not to give up. I went through a dark period. Weeks five and six, and then even the two or three weeks post-treatment, are the hardest, because the radiation continues to burn, even worse after it's over. Those are the darkest periods, as far as pain was concerned, but it showed me that I still had strength. I still could keep going and I would say, *If I could just make it home and get in that bed...*

Those were my daily goals, Nio, at the time. I mean, I'm serious, how simple it sounds, but you just can't wait to get out of your clothes that you wore that day and get in your bed and just cuddle up.

I had motivational books sent to me that I would read. That's very helpful, to read, people should read through that.

JOY NOTES

There's a book that a friend of mine gave me that truly was special, and my cousin, Carol, gave me a special book that's about someone who goes through cancer treatments. It's a daily motivational book and it's real, it's not like the fluff pie-in-the-sky kind of stuff. It truly is.

One day, the pain was so bad, I [asked God], *Just let me get through the pain of today and put me to sleep*, and those are the kinds of prayers that I was praying at the time. I'll tell you, going through all that changes everything about you—the way you look at people, the way you look at life, the way you look at tomorrow.

When I went back recently to find out if it's gone—which was probably the most emotional day—that day, and then the last day of treatment, was so emotional. I have videos . . . about when I rang the bell whenever [I had] the last treatment.

Nio: I want to definitely see you ring the bell. That's awesome.

Deb: I'll send that to you. When I went back for the CT scan, I thought that I would not get the results that same day. I thought it would be, like 48 hours, whatever. No, I went to have a CT scan at 2:00, and at 3:30, I went to see my oncologist, and she had the results right there. She'd already read them, and she said:

"It's gone. The tumors are gone. There's barely a trace that we can see on the lymph nodes and that, to me, puts a little bit of doubt in my mind, as they may come back and there's no guarantees."

There's no guarantees, but this has been the most effective treatment they found today, and I'm telling you, the survival rate 10 or 20 years ago for this type of cancer was just not what it is today. I feel blessed that I went to Vanderbilt University Medical Center to have treatment. It's a great facility for cancer treatment.

CHAPTER 9

Nio: Absolutely.

Deb: Surrounded by loved ones. That's kind of my journey in a nutshell.

Nio: What music did you listen to during this time? What's your genre?

Deb: It's called "Overcomer" by Mandisa on YouTube . . . you have to hear it and see it. It's just more of a visual and—

Nio: It's totally beautiful. I would say that it's contemporary.

Deb: You know Robin [Roberts] from the news [Good Morning America]? She fought through cancer. [There's a website that shows people, including her, who fought through cancer. It shows their journey. Here is the link: https://www.joincake.com/blog/famous-cancer-survivors/.]

Nio: Wow.

Deb: I played that so many times because of the words for me, and every word on that video she said was what I was fighting through. You got to watch the video and listen to the music, because it really is cool.

Nio: I was just watching a little piece of it and it was impressive. She has a beautiful voice, too.

Deb: Yeah, she sure does. That's one of the songs my sister sent me. I would get music sent to me from friends and family, and they were like, "Hey, listen to this song" ["When You Need It" by Tenille Townes featuring Wrabel]. My sister was probably the one who sent me most of them. They were motivational music, but I like all genres of music and I strayed away from the sad stuff. I would try to listen to things that were more uplifting and positive. That's one thing I would also recommend. I made a mistake one night by turning on some Adele.

Nio: Lord, what are you trying to do?

Deb: Back in the old days, whenever she made albums and I was angry [I would listen to her music and be okay with the lyrics that can be sad].

Nio: It's so funny, because I think about it through my illness journeys, too . . . and I've always stayed away from the adults. I've always stayed away from the tissue breakers and I always say, *Oh my God, why would we want to stay hugging the trauma instead of breaking through the trauma?*

Deb: I call those a pity party.

Nio: Yes, that's exactly what it is. I told myself when I was sick, *I'm giving you an hour of pity party a day*, because, like you said, I think you said it beautifully, the darkness creeps in. We can't avoid it. It's going to creep in when you're in pain.

Deb: Yes, that's right.

Nio: I said to myself, *You get an hour of pity party a day, and after that hour happens, you smack it on the nose like if it was a dog.*

Deb: That's right

Nio: And you keep on moving. Or punch it in the throat like if it's a human.

CHAPTER 9

Deb: That's right. Now, here's another song . . . My friend Beth, she lives in Nashville. She has been there for me from day one. This song is really about her and how I would get in those dark places and she would call me and remind me not to do that.

It's called "When You Need It" by Tenille Townes featuring Wrabel. That's a Country song, by the way. It tells you, when you need a friend, what not to do in a dark place. It's a great song, but that's the kind of stuff that I would listen to that would motivate me. My mother would send me some songs as well, or tell me some songs to play. But yeah, music does change your mood, or keep you in a mood. Music is very important to me because I am a musician. I love all kinds of music, but during that time it was hard. I play the piano. I'm a pianist.

Nio: Same as me.

Deb: Yeah, I've been playing since third grade. I don't have a piano right now. I actually gave my keyboard to my granddaughter and she's learning to play it, but I enjoy it.

Nio: Yeah, same here. I keep my keyboard in my office, because when I'm frustrated, I put those headphones on and I hit it hard.

Deb: That's right. Another thing is I have a craft, I knit and weave and all that stuff. Of course, at the time, I could not weave. I can't sit in the chair at a loom, because it wasn't comfortable for me, but **knitting was also a saving grace. I would lay in bed and knit, and that would take my mind off of things. It's just a repetitive thing that you're focused on that combats the pain and everything else around you. Knitting was important to me.**

Find a craft. Somebody find something that you like to do and take your mind off of it, but don't give up, just don't give up, that's all I can say. Don't give up.

That was my journey. It was hard, but I made it through, on the other side, and then I bought a Harley. I've always ridden motorcycles my whole life, and after I was diagnosed, I'm thinking, *I'll never be able to ride again because of the location of my cancer*, and I'm thinking, *You know what? I'm going to do it. I'm going to do it.* So I got back on and rode and I bought a Harley.

Nio: So happy for you on that, because I know how much you love to ride. I mean, back in Pennsylvania, we had some fun.

Deb: We did.

Nio: Just knowing that you went back to something you loved, and just knowing that you said to yourself, *this is for me*. We spend way too much time not acknowledging ourselves, and not giving ourselves grace to find our happy—nobody else's—but just ours. To see you go and ride, that's awesome. Good stuff.

Deb: One thing that I love to do, too, Nio, and you do, too, is that I love to cook. So not being able to do that throughout that time was hard for me. But I truly enjoyed when my older sons would come over and cook for me and prepare for me. Trey, my oldest, is just a great chef. He should have been a chef in his lifetime. He really should have been, because that's his calling.

Nio: There is still time; he can change his [career]. There's so many people who do. There's no reason. It's just such a hard life.

Deb: Yeah, it is. I know. We enjoy getting together and doing things as a family, and he would come over and cook soups for me because I didn't watch what I ate all the time.

CHAPTER 9

Nio: Right. You know what he can do? He can actually, now that you're doing better . . . he can search for his purpose freely.

Deb: That's true. I'm working on my store again. I've got the store built, and all that was done when I was sick. I couldn't focus on the builders and all that. I just let my children take that over, but now I'm focused back on that, and I'm having the flooring put down right now, I'm having some shelving built, and the bathroom being built out by my neighbor, so I'm hoping to get that done [soon].

Nio: That's perfect for you.

Deb: That's right.

Nio: I just think about how much I loved . . . the whole farm and going out there and spending the weekend, learning how to loom and all that.

Nio: I know how much you love to teach, and it is a great time with girls, and I'll load you up.

Deb: You know another idea somebody had, I think Beth told me, she's like, "All these people, they come to Nashville, these girls are getting married, they're having bachelorette parties, but now they're also having divorce parties. And these are older ladies."

Nio: Oh, my God. Yes.

Deb: Come to the farm and have a divorce party. Let's celebrate your divorce. It's stuff like that that I need to tap into—people's thoughts and ideas, and that'll be fun, too. I think 2024 is going to be a better year than 2023 for me, for sure. I had a sign in my bathroom that Beth gave me. It says "Shit Creek Survivor." You should title my chapter **Shit Creek Survivor**. I'll send you a picture of that little sign.

Nio: Send me a picture of the sign, because that is done. It'll be the subtitle of this chapter. It's an homage to you. You and I have been through so much.

Deb: I know. Oh, my gosh. We have. It's just been too much.

Nio: We've never given up.

Deb: No, we never did, and we won't.

Nio: We will never give up.

Deb: That's right.

Nio: We've always just supported each other in the midst of the craziest stuff that could happen to people for another day. We always have just moved forward, and the thing about the book, it's about women understanding that they're never alone.

Deb: Right.

Nio: They're never alone, and they will find refuge in those that they didn't expect to find refuge. It's that friend who hasn't talked to you in 10 years, but guess what? They're really a friend. Sometimes the one that's right next to you, isn't.

Deb: That's right.

Nio: Sometimes they're a negative, but it's the one who knew you 10 years ago who has a place in the heart for you no

CHAPTER 9

matter what, and they would ride or die for you. They don't have to be in your face every day.

Deb: Right. It's so funny, Nio, you say that, too. My two older boys, all three of them, really, recognized how many friends I have. It is overwhelming. And they all three said, "Mom, we didn't realize how nationwide your friendship goes."

I said, "Guys, you have to remember, I lived on the West Coast, I lived in Texas, I've worked all over the United States and India."

And they don't forget that. People reach out. Like I said, I heard from a high school friend of mine that I haven't heard from in 30 years, who reached out to me after he found out, and anyway, that was a blessing for me, too, and it was a treat to hear from people. Phone numbers come across; I don't even know who they were, and I'm like, *who is this phone number?*

This kept me going. And another thing, too, Nio, is that website, that journal blog that I put together, it's called CaringBridge.com, it's for health journeys for people who go through that. It's a daily blog [https://www.caring-bridge.org/visit/debrastall]. That's a good way to journal your thoughts, what you're going through. And recently, someone just found out that I had it, and now I'm clear, they wanted to hear about the journey. I said, just go read my blog, and you can do that, too. Nio. if you go back to my Caring Bridge, I'll send you a link to it so you can read from day one to whenever it was over and what all I went through. I mean, I had some dark posts on here, too, Nio.

Nio: It's okay. I think that people don't understand that part of our journey is dark, and you have to get through the darkness. That's why the book is called From Trauma to Triumph, and it's because the trauma is the darkness, and that means that we're going to have some moments that aren't pretty.

Deb: That's right. Well, that will also give you some more color around what I went through and there's, I think, 52 different journal entries that I did a journal for, and then I did one recently, too. I don't post much anymore because there's just really not much going on with my health, but it does show the path and the journey that I went through in that blog. I'm glad I did that because I'm writing a recipe book, it's not just recipes, it's things like these kids today don't know how to cook.

Nio: Know how to boil water, honey.

Deb: Right. My book is going to include how to make soap, how to make moonshine. I don't want it to die with our generation. All my recipes that I cook for my family, I want them to remember me by some of this stuff that I do. That's what I'm doing, and that blog, I'm going to pull some stuff from that, but I've got to get back to that. It's not been a focus of mine recently, but I need to do that in 2024.

Nio: You know what? You're doing a lot. Take your time. Do it with joy, and thank you for putting together those recipes. I've always enjoyed your food, and even when I'm not eating it directly, just watching your online posts always gives me joy. Don't stop. Like you say, never stop.

Deb: Never stop, never give up.

Nio: The fact of the matter is, this is your journey, you've touched so many people with your talents, all level of talents, that that's why I said to you this is just a way of you touching more people, and this will not hurt you, and it took those that needed to get out of your life, out.

CHAPTER 9

Deb: Right. My oncologist said, you got rid of the real cancer.

Nio: You got rid of the real cancer. Cancer, yes, straight up.

Deb: That's what my family said, too. They're like, you purged the real cancer.

Nio: Purged the real cancer out of your life. Now you're okay.

Deb: That's right. I'm happier than I've ever been in my life. I could lose a few pounds. I didn't have an appetite all through the treatments, but I started having an appetite, so I'm like, you know what? I would enjoy my joy, my tab. I'll do it again in 2024. I'll try to lose, but I'll be honest with you, I was taking those shots, not Ozempic, but it's the Wegovy, and that's what made me so constipated, Nio, and that's kind of what shed light on my whole cancer thing back in the early part of this year. I'm afraid to go back to those shots and do that again.

Nio: Well, I wouldn't do it. I mean, there's so many new reports, please don't do this to your body, people. The benefit is temporary because once you get off them, you blow up anyway.

Deb: Right. Exactly.

Nio: Why put yourself through all that for two weeks of cute? Because you're not learning anything. All you're doing is basically being constipated, being sick. Most people, it just tears up their stomach.

Deb: It does and it makes you nauseated, and it's just miserable for me.

Nio: I don't see the purpose.

Deb: I do need to eat better, and I've done it before just by eating the right things. Even through the treatments, I lost a lot of weight because it went right through me, and so they told me to eat a low fiber diet at the time, so I couldn't eat fresh greens and things like that, but now I can.

Nio: Right.

Deb: Anyway, this has been great. Thanks.

Nio: Now that you can walk around your farm with all the stuff that you do as you get your energy back up, you lose the weight naturally. You won't have to worry about it. Anyway, you cook very healthy, it's just doing a little exercise with it. You'll be fine.

Deb: Yeah, I had a Peloton bike, and I just couldn't ride that bike because of the cancer. I'm getting back on the motorcycle, so I'm going to get back on the peloton. I can do that now.

Nio: All right, thank you for this time.

DEB'S THREE TIPS FOR SURVIVING & THRIVING WITH JOY

Deb told her story, and shared tips for overcoming trauma and living joyously, regardless of your life circumstances. Everyone composes her own score for finding your *Joy Notes*, and here is hers:

CHAPTER 9

1. **Play a musical instrument.** She plays piano, and loses herself in the rapture of her fingers dancing across the keyboard and her senses getting lost in the pleasure of hearing the music that she's playing. The act of playing music is a wonderful distraction from worry, fear, anxiety, and pain.

    Playing a musical instrument forces the brain to focus on the tremendous mental energy required to recall memorized music, read sheet music, play the correct piano keys, coordinate breathing and finger movements on wind instruments, striking the right guitar strings, move the bow with perfect precision on a string instrument such as a violin, and synchronize hand/foot coordination on a drum set or organ. Playing a musical instrument has a spiritual component, as the energy and flow can feel as if you're connected to an energy greater than yourself that's allowing the creation of beautiful music that mellows you and delights your senses as well as those of anyone who's listening.

2. **Have a craft.** Deb relaxed and took her mind off of her health crisis by indulging her passion for knitting and weaving. The repetitive motions lulled her mind while her brain energy focused on the mechanical movements of her fingers as they used the needles to loop the yarn, or maneuvered the loom to create a tapestry. She also enjoyed time reading and cooking.

3. **Surround yourself with loved ones and rely on them for help.** Deb's devoted circle of friends and family members were her saving grace. They brought her food, kept her company, encouraged her, checked on her, and helped her stay positive. This was especially important after her partner abruptly abandoned her without saying goodbye

after she announced that she had rectal cancer. Don't be too proud to ask for and receive the help that you need. Be gracious and grateful to everyone who shares even the smallest gesture, because every moment and every kindness all adds up to your healing and continued wellness.

If you're enduring a health challenge, don't be afraid to call on your friends and family to help you. And if you have a friend or family member who is ailing, please let Deb's story inspire you to be there for that person; the rays of sunshine that you shine on them through your kindness can help them survive and thrive.

CHAPTER 10

Songstress Gloria Gaynor Says You Will Survive!

*D*isco: A musical genre that grew out of America's urban nightlife scene during the 1970s, characterized by a fast, repetitive beat with electric guitars and piano, synthesizers, horns and brass, and strings.

Gloria Gaynor's global hit song, "I Will Survive," has lifted me from the lowest lows of my life, both emotional and physical, and I consider this the ultimate anthem for women's empowerment. The lyrics are the perfect expression of the internal fortitude and faith that I and the others have shared in this book.

When the inspiration to write *Joy Notes* filled my heart, my first thought was the anthem of women's strength: "I Will Survive" by Gloria Gaynor. She has won two Grammy Awards and she has been nominated for music's highest honor seven times. And I thought, *I must ask Gloria Gaynor to write the Foreword.*

It had been ages since I connected with Gloria, so I asked Darcel, a mutual dear friend, to reach out to the famous songstress on my behalf to inquire about writing the Foreword for *Joy Notes*. A short time later, I had the privilege and pleasure of interviewing Gloria.

"The book is not only about telling the stories, but also about telling how music plays a role in us pulling through," I told her, "because **we can't pull through without having a song in our hearts**. The song changes during the stages of our heart, but there is that song that when you hear it, you're like, *Yes, girl, I got you. Yeah. I'm good. I'm good. I'm all right.*"

I told Gloria that Darcel shares her story in this book, and that every woman has her personal song that inspires her *Joy Notes* to help her balance the trauma with triumph.

"I'm a Disco kid," I told Gloria. "We all are. There is some Rock, some Jazz, and all genres. Of course, I have my Salsa, with the Cuban in there, too. The book flows through music. This book comes from my heart and it's my mission to do this."

Gloria's contribution to this book is so special because the era when she lit up the world with her song—the late 1970s—was a time of creating identity and innovation. Electronic rhythms and voices explored new dimensions. Explosive dance music created the phenomenon of Discotheques.

Can you hear it? The sound coming out of Studio 54 in NYC electrified the world and became a legendary icon of that time. The red velvet rope—which held back those who were not allowed to enter, and opened for those who were—was invented to facilitate the discriminating selection of who was flashy, cool, or beautiful enough to enter the magic of Studio 54 and other clubs. At the tine, I was entering my teens—not old enough to enter such places—but completely fascinated with the world of Disco. The music was captivating and the artists were mesmerizing.

As a young Black woman, it was incredible to see such talent that looked like *me*—making history! This ranged from

CHAPTER 10

Gloria Gaynor setting it off with "Never Can Say Goodbye" in 1974, then opening the door to Donna Summer, Grace Jones, and Diana Ross, to creating the Disco anthem of "I Will Survive" that is still played in every country at every club.

This music was my "you can do all things" beat. It gave us the chance to be free and capable of all things. The music was about empowerment. The female artists wrote their songs with stories of drama, awareness, resiliency, and the heroine overcoming the worst challenges. We were surviving, working hard for the money, coming out—slaves to the rhythm, dancing through our days and nights as these *Joy Notes* struck chords of happiness and better health in our hearts and souls.

I loved Disco dancing, and my hustle partner was my oldest brother when he was home. I loved learning all the moves that I saw on "Dance Fever," a syndicated variety TV show that featured Disco dancers and celebrities who competed every week. (It was the first iteration of the "Dancing with the Stars" concept.)

It was amazing to watch Deney Terrio and his backup dancers rule the world with Disco. My brother Rafale was a perfectionist; he practiced two to three hours a day, and his goal was to make it on "Dance Fever." He went to all the discotheques where the scouts visited to find new dancers. He also went to open calls, which he could quickly do because he lived across from New York City. Dancing was his passion.

His perseverance did not go in vain; he was finally selected for the show and made it on the show in 1981. This was his second time on stage dancing on TV. His first was on "SOUL TRAIN" when our local Memorial High School was featured. Rafael was a phenomenal dancer, artist, and IT professional.

My brother passed in April 2022, two months to the day from the death of my father. Like my dad, he was a brilliant artist who lived life fully. He lived life like Disco, making sure that every moment counted for something. If there was breath in him, everything was designed to make a difference.

Disco taught him that you have to be great to something new but only by starting can you get to become great. His mindset was always based on the mantra, *Don't just exist; live fully.* That is the essence of Disco. It started from nothing and blossomed into a culture that opened the door to new musical genres such as House Music and Funk.

Gloria Gaynor's Health Crisis Showcased Her Surviving Spirit
Here's how she tells the story:

I had fallen on stage during a performance at the Beacon Theater. I had this skit in the show during which I would take the microphone by the head with the cord across the stage to my two male background singers. We'd been through a total war with the microphone cord. I'm telling you this now, but this doesn't have anything to do with the song. But anyway, I would do that. So, this particular night, I whipped the cord across the stage. They picked it up, but they didn't hold it.

So, when I pulled on it to do the tug-of-war bit, there was no tension and I fell backwards over the monitor behind me. But I jumped back up and finished the show. I went out to breakfast with a group afterward and went home and went to sleep. I woke up the next morning paralyzed from the waist down.

They called an ambulance. First of all, I was able to move my arm, so I called my then-boyfriend and told him that I was paralyzed. He called the ambulance and then came over. He said by the time he got there, just before the ambulance arrived, I was screaming at the top of my lungs. I don't remember. They took me to the hospital and I was in the hospital for three-and-a-half months.

CHAPTER 10

I did all kinds of testing and procedures and finally ended up with surgery where they fused my two bones in my lumbar. When I came out of the hospital, I had lost everything—my apartment, my furniture, everything. And I went to stay with my boyfriend because I had nowhere else to go.

"I don't do the shacking up thing," I told him. "Either I get on my feet and get out of here, or we're getting married. I didn't grow up like that."

That ended the relationship.

Gloria prayed for God to lift her up and out of this crisis, and a short time later, she was presented with the song that elevated her to an iconic and beloved songstress.

"I Will Survive" provided the words she needed to rise up and out of her health crisis and break-up, and became her gift to the world to help people everywhere do the same.

The song was inducted into the U.S. Library of Congress' National Recording Registry in 2016. In addition, Gloria Gaynor was awarded an Honorary Degree of Doctor of Music from Dowling College in 2015. She received the "Legend" Award at the World Music Awards in Monte Carlo in 2022. She's also a recipient of the Martin Luther King, Jr. Award, and many others. She continues to perform around the world.

Amazing, as this book went to press, a documentary about her life was shown in theatres on February 13, 2024, and the top media programs including NPR and *The Today Show* featured interviews with her.

Learn more at GloriaGaynor.com.

JOY NOTES

GLORIA'S THREE TIPS FOR SURVIVING & THRIVING WITH JOY

Here are Gloria Gaynor's tips on how to overcome and live joyously:

• **Don't underestimate yourself.**
Have faith that God will orchestrate events that lift you up and out of your trauma. Gloria prayed and believed that God would make something great happen in her career, even when her record company had said it would not renew her contract. Then the opposite happened, they renewed her and she was presented with the opportunity to record a song that brought global success and made her a beloved icon of women's empowerment and Disco joy.

• **Recognize success when you see it, and believe in its infinite potential, even when others don't.**
Gloria knew she was looking at a hit song as soon as she read the lyrics of "I Will Survive." Even though this global sensation was the B-side of another record that she didn't even like. Then she took the records to Studio 54 herself and gave them to the DJs to play on the radio. That took hutzpah, courage, confidence, and unwavering belief in herself and the power of this song.

• **Know the healing power of music.**
Gloria's hit song, "I Will Survive," resonated so deeply with her on a personal level—as she read the lyrics for the first time—that she began to heal. She saw her own story in the song, and it affirmed her power to persevere through the pain. The confidence-boosting message in her song,

along with the joyous beat, struck the hearts, minds, and bodies of people in discoes and through the airwaves across New York, but encouraging them to survive the toughest circumstances. The healing power of "I Will Survive" is immeasurable and iconic.

Disco Plays Our Joy Notes

Gloria Gaynor came through paralysis and lost everything that she valued. Even her recording contract was in jeopardy.

That season of life made her aware of the power of faith, perseverance, following your gut, and working harder than others are willing to do because the vision is clear and the difference it will make is greater than your personal comfort. Gloria understood that she had to focus her energy on her success—not on anyone who didn't care for her. She's never stopped moving onward and upward, and continues today to uplift and inspire people around the world.

Gloria Gaynor and other Disco artists give us the ability to understand that we can be our own heroes, and that drama only defines a moment not who we are. The lyrics reminds us that we can't stop looking forward if we are going to make it to the other side.

I am invigorated every time I listen to Disco, the beat makes me dance, I sing non-stop, and I feel unstoppable. So put a little Disco into your life when things seem bleak.

And also remember to play your *Joy Notes* to cope with pain and create a life that you love.

ABOUT THE AUTHOR

Niobis Queiro

After working in the healthcare industry for more than 30 years, Nio unexpectedly stepped into the role of patient in 2021.

She was at the salon getting her hair done when she started experiencing excruciating abdominal pain. She was rushed to the hospital, where she was diagnosed with an abdominal obstruction and sepsis. Despite multiple near-death experiences during surgery and treatment, Nio survived and made a full recovery.

Now, on the other side of the healing process, and equipped with a new perspective on vulnerability, resilience, and the value of community, Nio is determined to empower and inspire others to live with meaning.

Nio is a certified energy leadership practitioner who uses her coaching education, executive healthcare background, and life experience to help individuals and teams connect with their authentic selves, set and achieve goals, and cultivate a culture of community.

Invite Nio Queiro to Speak

Create an unforgettable and transformative experience at your next event...

When you invite celebrated speaker Nio Quiero to share her inspiring messages for companies, corporations, organizations, colleges and universities, nonprofits, and fundraisers.

She can provide motivational speaking and/or training sessions to help people discover joy and purpose in one's professional and personal lives.

Nio is an executive coach and speaker who is continuously evolving her expertise around diverse subjects. Here is a sampling of her main topics:

1. Diversity, Equity, Inclusion, and Belonging in the healthcare and workforce setting.

2. Chameleon Communication: How to enhance your communication skills to influence your audience and be impactful in your professional exchanges by using the best body language, mastering your voice speed and tone, and creating a connection with your listener.

3. Leadership Boot Camp: Learn the skills of effective leadership through empathy, honor, motivation, transparency, and vulnerability.

4. Women's Empowerment: Understand the power within and know how to use it to accomplish your goals with purpose.

5. Innovation Culture Creation: Establish an organizational mindset of innovation that celebrates failure as a catalyst to success.

Include a book signing at your event

Joy Notes is available for bulk discount orders to provide

ABOUT THE AUTHOR

every participant with a copy of this life-changing book.

Order the book at TwoSistersWriting.com.

Joy Notes features a Foreword by Grammy Award Winning Artist Gloria Gaynor, best known for her 1978 hit, "I Will Survive." The book shares Nio's remarkable life story and miraculous recovery from the brink of death. Because she finds healing in music, each chapter highlights a musical genre as well as interviews with amazing women whose stories and lessons—along with Nio's—provide tips and guidance for living an empowered life, especially when dealing with health crises.

When Nio speaks, she can autograph books. She's also available for a private dinner with the author for select participants who can also benefit from a small group coaching session.

To invite Nio to speak, please submit a request at:

www.queirogroup.com

PLAYLIST for JOY NOTES

CHAPTER	SONGS	SINGER
FOREWORD	I WILL SURVIVE	GLORIA GAYNOR
Chapter 1	Yo Tengo Gozo en Mi Alma	Alabare
	Don't Stop Believin'	Journey
	We Are the Champions	Queen
	Chariots Of Fire	Vangelis
	Fur Elise	Ludwig van Beethoven
	Etude Op. 10 (Waterfall)	Fryderyk Chopin
	Clair de Lune	Claude Debussy
	UnPretty	TLC
	Wonder Woman Theme Song	Norman Gimbel and Charles Fox
Chapter 2	Buena Vista Social Club	Buena Vista Social Club
	Gusto Y Sabor	Vieja Trova Santiaguera
	Para Los Bailadores	Septeto Santiaguero
	Me Olvide de Vivir	Julio Iglesias
	Amor	Julio Iglesias
	Guantanamera	Celia Cruz
	Rie y Llora	Celia Cruz
	Asi Es Beny	Benny Moré
	Oye Como Va	Celia Cruz
Chapter 3	Woman You Must Be Crazy	T-Bone Walker
	It's Your Breath in Our Lungs	Eddie James
	Stand and Fight	James Taylor
	Slippin' In	Buddy Guy
	Tell It Like It Is	Aaron Neville
Chapter 4	Rapper's Delight	The Sugarhill Gang
	Superappin'	Grandmaster Flash, Furious Five, Melle Mel
	To the Beat Y'All	Lady B
	U.N.I.T.Y.	Queen Latifah
	I Can't Live Without My Radio	LL Cool J
Chapter 5	Gimme Shelter	The Rolling Stones
	Scars in Heaven	Casting Crowns
	Keep Your Hands to Yourself	The Georgia Satellites
	Every Day is Exactly the Same	Nine Inch Nails
	Erase My Scars	Evans Blue
	More Than Words	Extreme
Chapter 6	Tango	Dianne Reeves
	Calm Before the Storm	Jonathan Butler
	Falling in Love with Jesus	Jonathan Butler
	Ascension (Don't Ever Wonder)	Maxwell
	By Your Side	Sade
	You'll Never Walk Alone	Nina Simone
Chapter 7	You've Got a Friend	James Taylor
	Crazy	Patsy Cline
	Jolene	Dolly Parton
	Fancy	Reba McEntire
	Goodbye Earl	The Chicks
	I Walk the Line	Johnny Cash and The Tennessee Two
Chapter 8	Uptown Funk	Mark Ronson featuring Bruno Mars
	We Will Rock You	Queen
	I Won't Back Down	Tom Petty
	Livin' on a Prayer	Bon Jovi
	Confident	Demi Lovato
	I'm All Right	Kenny Loggins
Chapter 9	Whatever It Takes	Imagine Dragons and Jorgen Odegard
	When You Need it	Tenille Townes
	Overcomer	Mandisa
	One Moment in Time	Whitney Houston
	Winning	Carlos Santana
	I'm Still Standing	Elton John
Chapter 10	I Will Survive	Gloria Gaynor
	Never Can Say Goodbye	Gloria Gaynor
	(If You Want It) Do It Yourself	Gloria Gaynor
	Ain't No Stoppin' Us Now	McFadden & Whitehead
	Stayin' Alive	Bee Gees
	You Make Me Feel (Mighty Real)	Sylvester
	I'm Every Woman	Chaka Khan

Endnotes

[1] "I Will Survive," Wikipedia, last modified 07 February 2024, https://en.wikipedia.org/wiki/I_Will_Survive

[2] "Quote by J.D. Salinger," Goodreads, https://www.goodreads.com/quotes/13805-the-fact-is-always-obvious-much-too-late-but-the

[3] "Blues," Dictionary, Google, https://www.google.com/search?q=the+blues+definition&oq=the+blues+definition&gs_lcrp=EgZjaHJvbWUyBggAEEUYOdIBCDM4MjNqMGo3qAIAsAIA&sourceid=chrome&ie=UTF-8

[4] https://en.wikipedia.org/wiki/Jazz

[5] "Jazz," Wikipedia, last modified 9 February 2024, https://en.wikipedia.org/wiki/Jazz

[6] Sara Henning-Stout, "Laughter as Medicine: Humor Therapy Reduces Depression and Anxiety Symptoms," Neuroscience News, June 21, 2023, https://neurosciencenews.com/humor-therapy-depression-24507/

Printed in the USA
CPSIA information can be obtained
at www.ICGtesting.com
CBHW020242030424
6256CB00003B/3